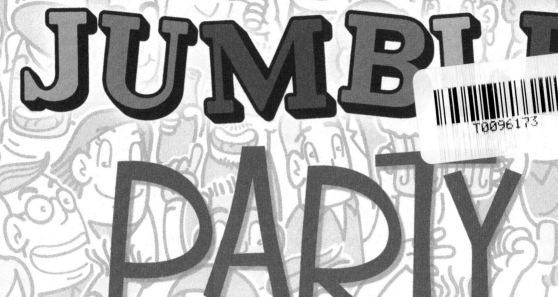

JUMBLE PARTY

**Henri Arnold,
Bob Lee,
David L. Hoyt
and Jeff Knurek**

TRIUMPH
BOOKS

For further information, con tact:
Triumph Books LLC
814 North Franklin Street
Chicago, Illinois 60610
Phone: (312) 337-0747
www.triumphbooks.com

Printed in U.S.A.

ISBN: 978-1-63727-008-0

Design by Sue Knopf

Contents

Classic Puzzles
1–25...Page 1

Daily Puzzles
26–160...Page 27

Challenger Puzzles
161–180...Page 163

Answers
Page 184

JUMBLE® PARTY

Classic Puzzles

JUMBLE®

Unscramble these four Jumbles, one letter
to each square, to form four ordinary words.

LYSHY

GOBEF

SLATTE

RUPPLE

WHAT JOKES TOLD
BY AN ABDOMINAL
SURGEON ARE APT
TO BE.

Now arrange the circled letters
to form the surprise answer, as
suggested by the above cartoon.

**Print answer
here**

JUMBLE®

Unscramble these four Jumbles, one letter
to each square, to form four ordinary words.

NAGIT

COHLT

PAMNEC

RASTUX

THE ARTIST WENT
TO THE PICTURE
FRAME SHOP
BECAUSE HE HAD SO
MANY OF THESE.

Now arrange the circled letters
to form the surprise answer, as
suggested by the above cartoon.

Print answer here ⬡⬡⬡⬡ – ⬡⬡⬡

JUMBLE®

Unscramble these four Jumbles, one letter to each square, to form four ordinary words.

HIGEW

DEUXE

VESSUR

FONZER

WHY SHE LIKED THE GUY WHO ALWAYS BROUGHT STALE BREAD.

Now arrange the circled letters to form the surprise answer, as suggested by the above cartoon.

Print answer here

HE ⬡⬡⬡⬡⬡ GOT " ⬡⬡⬡⬡⬡ "

JUMBLE®

Unscramble these four Jumbles, one letter to each square, to form four ordinary words.

SAYID

RADAW

THIRDE

BEFLAD

WHICH SIDE OF THE FIRE IS THE HOTTEST?

Now arrange the circled letters to form the surprise answer, as suggested by the above cartoon.

Print answer here THE " ⬡⬡⬡⬡ ⬡⬡⬡⬡ "

JUMBLE®

Unscramble these four Jumbles, one letter
to each square, to form four ordinary words.

ORRMA

ARBSS

TENAGE

RUBBUS

WHAT A BACKSEAT
DRIVER NEVER DOES,
UNFORTUNATELY.

Now arrange the circled letters
to form the surprise answer, as
suggested by the above cartoon.

☐☐☐☐ ☐☐☐ OF " ☐☐☐ "

JUMBLE®

Unscramble these four Jumbles, one letter
to each square, to form four ordinary words.

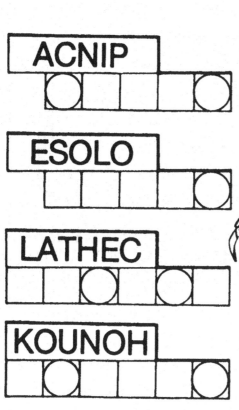

ACNIP

ESOLO

LATHEC

KOUNOH

WHAT CAP IS
NEVER REMOVED?

Now arrange the circled letters
to form the surprise answer, as
suggested by the above cartoon.

Print answer here THE

JUMBLE®

Unscramble these four Jumbles, one letter
to each square, to form four ordinary words.

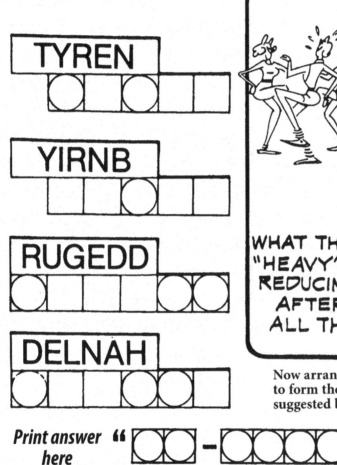

TYREN

YIRNB

RUGEDD

DELNAH

WHAT THE FORMERLY
"HEAVY" CLIENT AT THE
REDUCING SALON SAID
AFTER SHE LOST
ALL THAT WEIGHT.

Now arrange the circled letters
to form the surprise answer, as
suggested by the above cartoon.

*Print answer
here* " ☐☐ - ☐☐☐☐☐☐ - ☐☐ "

JUMBLE®

Unscramble these four Jumbles, one letter to each square, to form four ordinary words.

NOOZE

HECKE

DUNTIC

WIMDLE

WHAT THE PILLOW
TYCOON GOT
WHEN BUSINESS
WAS BAD.

Now arrange the circled letters to form the surprise answer, as suggested by the above cartoon.

Print answer here " ☐☐☐☐ " IN THE ☐☐☐☐☐☐

JUMBLE®

Unscramble these four Jumbles, one letter
to each square, to form four ordinary words.

NALAB

CONTH

PORTSY

GRACIT

OFFICE SUPPLIES

WHEN PRICES ON
EVERYTHING ELSE
WENT UP AT THAT
STORE, ENVELOPES
REMAINED THIS.

Now arrange the circled letters
to form the surprise answer, as
suggested by the above cartoon.

Print
answer
here   "   "

JUMBLE®

Unscramble these four Jumbles, one letter to each square, to form four ordinary words.

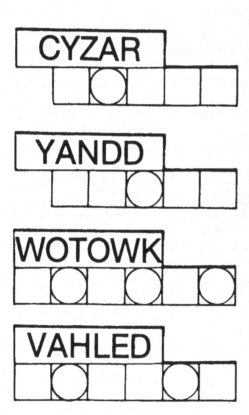

CYZAR

YANDD

WOTOWK

VAHLED

Drink up, everybody—
it's all on me!

HE SPENT HIS
MONEY LIKE WATER
BUT NOT THIS.

Now arrange the circled letters
to form the surprise answer, as
suggested by the above cartoon.

Print answer here

JUMBLE®

Unscramble these four Jumbles, one letter
to each square, to form four ordinary words.

HOOTT

TABLO

MEUGLE

CROSCH

WHERE GRAVE
ROBBERS LEARN
THEIR PROFESSION.

Now arrange the circled letters
to form the surprise answer, as
suggested by the above cartoon.

Print
answer
here

IN ⬡⬡⬡⬡⬡ ⬡⬡⬡⬡⬡⬡

JUMBLE®

Unscramble these four Jumbles, one letter to each square, to form four ordinary words.

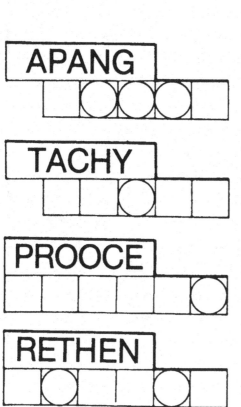

APANG

TACHY

PROOCE

RETHEN

WHAT SHE WANTED TO HEAR WHEN HE ASKED HER TO SHARE HIS LOT IN LIFE.

Now arrange the circled letters to form the surprise answer, as suggested by the above cartoon.

Print answer here THE

13

JUMBLE®

Unscramble these four Jumbles, one letter to each square, to form four ordinary words.

EJYTT

SCAIB

YELMOP

DOURNA

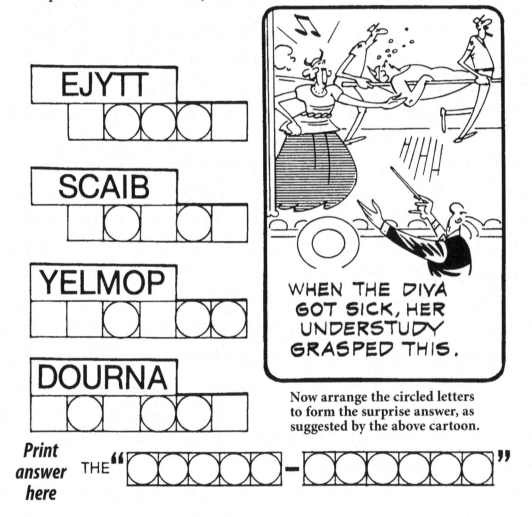

WHEN THE DIVA GOT SICK, HER UNDERSTUDY GRASPED THIS.

Now arrange the circled letters to form the surprise answer, as suggested by the above cartoon.

Print answer here THE " ◯◯◯◯◯ – ◯◯◯◯◯◯ "

JUMBLE®

Unscramble these four Jumbles, one letter
to each square, to form four ordinary words.

KARCC

RORYS

RAFTLE

PITTEE

MUST HAVE BEEN
A BIG WHEEL IN
THE AMUSEMENT
BUSINESS.

Now arrange the circled letters
to form the surprise answer, as
suggested by the above cartoon.

Print answer here

JUMBLE®

Unscramble these four Jumbles, one letter
to each square, to form four ordinary words.

NISEG

UNAFA

SIMDAL

YIBOSH

AN ANGLER EITHER
HAS FISH LYING
ABOUT HIM OR
HE'S THIS.

Now arrange the circled letters
to form the surprise answer, as
suggested by the above cartoon.

*Print answer
here* ⬡⬡⬡⬡⬡ ABOUT ⬡⬡⬡⬡

JUMBLE®

Unscramble these four Jumbles, one letter to each square, to form four ordinary words.

ACHOM

ONSIE

GRUEFE

THINEW

AN ARGUMENTATIVE PERSON IS NEVER SO FRUSTRATED AS WHEN YOU DO THIS.

Now arrange the circled letters to form the surprise answer, as suggested by the above cartoon.

Print answer here ◯◯◯◯◯ ◯◯◯◯ HIM

JUMBLE®

Unscramble these four Jumbles, one letter to each square, to form four ordinary words.

UPOHC

SCUFO

YARBET

MIRADS

STATIONERY

IF YOU HAVE AN ITCH TO WRITE, GET YOURSELF THIS.

Now arrange the circled letters to form the surprise answer, as suggested by the above cartoon.

Print answer here A ⬡⬡⬡⬡⬡⬡⬡ ⬡⬡⬡

18

JUMBLE

Unscramble these four Jumbles, one letter
to each square, to form four ordinary words.

NUCOE

DORRA

STUMEK

CHOPON

REPENT

THAT FANATIC GOES
THROUGH LIFE WITH
A CLOSED MIND
AND THIS.

Now arrange the circled letters
to form the surprise answer, as
suggested by the above cartoon.

Print answer here AN ☐☐☐☐☐ ☐☐☐☐☐

JUMBLE®

Unscramble these four Jumbles, one letter to each square, to form four ordinary words.

INYAR

THOOP

LISGRY

HINEAL

WHAT THE RECIPE FOR THIS COURSE REQUIRES A GREAT DEAL OF.

Now arrange the circled letters to form the surprise answer, as suggested by the above cartoon.

Print answer here " "

JUMBLE®

Unscramble these four Jumbles, one letter
to each square, to form four ordinary words.

DYNAS

SABIN

DELGEP

URKEEB

What a
lovely
day

It'll
probably
rain

IN THE SPRING THE
SKY SOMETIMES
SEEMS TO DO THIS.

Now arrange the circled letters
to form the surprise answer, as
suggested by the above cartoon.

Print answer here ⬡⬡⬡⬡⬡⬡ A ⬡⬡⬡⬡

JUMBLE®

Unscramble these four Jumbles, one letter
to each square, to form four ordinary words.

NAALC

DADIE

YISMAL

DORRIT

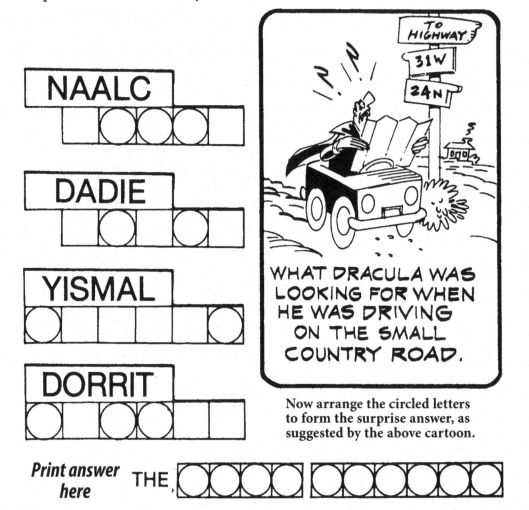

WHAT DRACULA WAS
LOOKING FOR WHEN
HE WAS DRIVING
ON THE SMALL
COUNTRY ROAD.

Now arrange the circled letters
to form the surprise answer, as
suggested by the above cartoon.

Print answer here THE, ⟨◯◯◯◯⟩ ⟨◯◯◯◯◯◯⟩

JUMBLE®

Unscramble these four Jumbles, one letter to each square, to form four ordinary words.

LATAN
◯ ◯ ◯ ◯ ◯

BIGEE
◯ ◯ ◯ ◯

GRAULF
◯ ◯ ◯ ◯ ◯ ◯

ROUVED
◯ ◯ ◯ ◯ ◯ ◯

Let's go, you guys!

HE WAS CHOSEN TO LEAD THE CREW TO OUTER SPACE, BE-CAUSE HE COULD BE TRUSTED TO KEEP THIS.

Now arrange the circled letters to form the surprise answer, as suggested by the above cartoon.

Print answer here

HIS ◯◯◯◯◯ ON THE ◯◯◯◯◯◯◯

JUMBLE®

Unscramble these four Jumbles, one letter to each square, to form four ordinary words.

EWLEH

TYLFO

BROWDY

KOHOED

HOW THE BULL SHOWED DEFERENCE TO HIS MATE.

Now arrange the circled letters to form the surprise answer, as suggested by the above cartoon.

Print answer here HE " ⬚⬚⬚ – ⬚⬚⬚⬚⬚ "

JUMBLE®

Unscramble these four Jumbles, one letter
to each square, to form four ordinary words.

SUGIE

THALC

UMDIBE

RETHOX

SICK
CALL
— —
Hours
— —

WHAT IT WAS WHEN
HE FAKED A
SPRAINED ANKLE.

Now arrange the circled letters
to form the surprise answer, as
suggested by the above cartoon.

Print answer here   A

JUMBLE®

Unscramble these four Jumbles, one letter
to each square, to form four ordinary words.

UPSIO

WREEF

RYSHER

SMUCLY

WHAT THE POLITICIAN
WAS WHEN THE
TELEPROMPTER
FAILED TO WORK.

Now arrange the circled letters
to form the surprise answer, as
suggested by the above cartoon.

Print answer here

JUMBLE ®

PARTY

Daily
Puzzles

JUMBLE®

Unscramble these four Jumbles, one letter to each square, to form four ordinary words.

MODEN

LALIV

TREFER

ITHELB

This is our hostess, Herbert— mind your p's and q's

WHAT SHE TRIED TO DO AFTER SHE MAR- RIED THAT CRUDE OIL BILLIONAIRE.

Now arrange the circled letters to form the surprise answer, as suggested by the above cartoon.

Print answer here

JUMBLE®

Unscramble these four Jumbles, one letter to each square, to form four ordinary words.

DESOU

SBELS

ONNIGG

BELEEF

BEFORE SHOES CAN BE BOUGHT THEY MUST BE THIS.

Now arrange the circled letters to form the surprise answer, as suggested by the above cartoon.

Print answer here "  "

JUMBLE®

Unscramble these four Jumbles, one letter
to each square, to form four ordinary words.

ZAWLT

CLOON

SOOMER

DOUSIT

WHO SAW THE
DINOSAUR ENTERING
THE RESTAURANT?

Now arrange the circled letters
to form the surprise answer, as
suggested by the above cartoon.

Print answer here   THE ⬡⬡⬡⬡⬡⬡⬡ ⬡⬡⬡

JUMBLE®

Unscramble these four Jumbles, one letter
to each square, to form four ordinary words.

BITHA
☐☐☐◯◯

RIVOS
☐◯◯◯◯

ENSICC
◯☐☐◯☐☐

YARDOP
◯☐☐◯◯☐

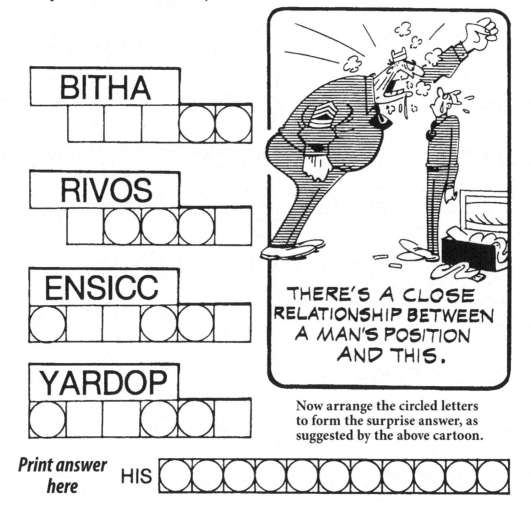

THERE'S A CLOSE
RELATIONSHIP BETWEEN
A MAN'S POSITION
AND THIS.

Now arrange the circled letters
to form the surprise answer, as
suggested by the above cartoon.

**Print answer
here**   HIS ◯◯◯◯◯◯◯◯◯◯◯◯

JUMBLE®

Unscramble these four Jumbles, one letter
to each square, to form four ordinary words.

WONGI

GLOIC

RAPPOL

CALVEE

MEANT THE
DISAPPEARANCE OF
THE CARRIAGE.

Now arrange the circled letters
to form the surprise answer, as
suggested by the above cartoon.

Print answer here   THE " ⬚⬚⬚ ⬚⬚⬚ "

JUMBLE®

Unscramble these four Jumbles, one letter
to each square, to form four ordinary words.

FAHFC

CEDID

GALLOB

INJOUR

Let's join the activities!

A STICK-IN-THE-MUD
FOUND IN A SHIP.

Now arrange the circled letters
to form the surprise answer, as
suggested by the above cartoon.

Print answer here   THE ⬡⬡⬡⬡⬡⬡

JUMBLE®

Unscramble these four Jumbles, one letter
to each square, to form four ordinary words.

GEDEW

ISSAB

CUIMPE

ZARQUT

WHAT TANTRUMS
ARE FOR SOME
KIDS THESE DAYS.

Now arrange the circled letters
to form the surprise answer, as
suggested by the above cartoon.

Print answer here ⬡⬡⬡⬡⬡⬡ THE ⬡⬡⬡⬡

JUMBLE®

Unscramble these four Jumbles, one letter to each square, to form four ordinary words.

CORUC

TOSOP

DUMPIO

HIRDBY

WHEN IT COMES TO LOVE, AN ENGAGEMENT RING IS THIS.

Now arrange the circled letters to form the surprise answer, as suggested by the above cartoon.

Print answer here   A "⬭⬭⬭⬭" ⬭⬭⬭⬭⬭⬭⬭

JUMBLE®

Unscramble these four Jumbles, one letter
to each square, to form four ordinary words.

AMFER

POAYS

YAQUES

RECHOM

DID YOU HEAR
MY LAST JOKE?

Now arrange the circled letters
to form the surprise answer, as
suggested by the above cartoon.

Print
answer
here

" I ⬡⬡⬡⬡ ⬡⬡⬡⬡ ⬡⬡ "

JUMBLE®

Unscramble these four Jumbles, one letter
to each square, to form four ordinary words.

DEWUN

HOTBO

SMOIGE

LOEPPE

Don't ever darken my door again!

WHAT A GUY WHO
ACTS LIKE A HEEL
SHOULD BE.

Now arrange the circled letters
to form the surprise answer, as
suggested by the above cartoon.

Print answer here

JUMBLE®

Unscramble these four Jumbles, one letter
to each square, to form four ordinary words.

TAIMY

HAWRT

NETOED

DECSON

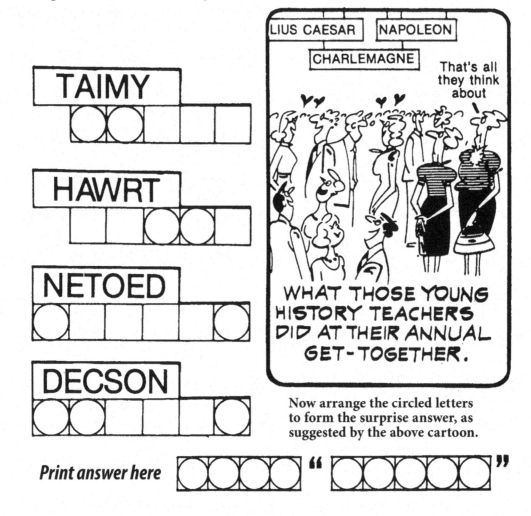

LIUS CAESAR   NAPOLEON
CHARLEMAGNE

That's all
they think
about

WHAT THOSE YOUNG
HISTORY TEACHERS
DID AT THEIR ANNUAL
GET-TOGETHER.

Now arrange the circled letters
to form the surprise answer, as
suggested by the above cartoon.

Print answer here ⬜⬜⬜⬜ " ⬜⬜⬜⬜⬜ "

JUMBLE®

Unscramble these four Jumbles, one letter
to each square, to form four ordinary words.

NIGTY
◻◻◯◯◯

SHACO
◻◯◻◻◻

ENBATE
◻◯◻◯◻◻

BLOWEB
◯◻◻◻◯◻

HOW PEOPLE SAW
THINGS AFTER THE
DISCOVERY OF
ELECTRICITY.

Now arrange the circled letters
to form the surprise answer, as
suggested by the above cartoon.

Print answer here IN A ◯◯◯◯ ◯◯◯◯◯

JUMBLE®

Unscramble these four Jumbles, one letter
to each square, to form four ordinary words.

SESMY

REGUP

BYRBAC

PHANEP

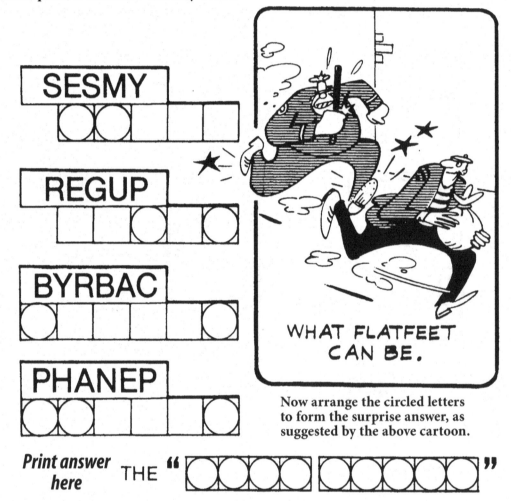

WHAT FLATFEET
CAN BE.

Now arrange the circled letters
to form the surprise answer, as
suggested by the above cartoon.

Print answer
here   THE " ◯◯◯◯◯ ◯◯◯◯◯◯ "

PUZZLE

39

JUMBLE®

Unscramble these four Jumbles, one letter
to each square, to form four ordinary words.

RUTYL

SONOW

UPDELD

CALARI

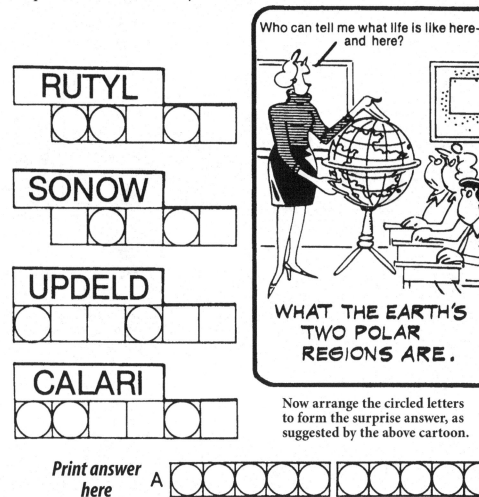

Who can tell me what life is like here—
and here?

WHAT THE EARTH'S
TWO POLAR
REGIONS ARE.

Now arrange the circled letters
to form the surprise answer, as
suggested by the above cartoon.

Print answer
here A ⬡⬡⬡⬡⬡⬡ ⬡⬡⬡⬡⬡

JUMBLE®

Unscramble these four Jumbles, one letter to each square, to form four ordinary words.

LARNG

NOPER

KIELLY

DEGURT

Opportunity knocked, but he was asleep

A GUY WHO HAS THE RIGHT AIM IN LIFE SOMETIMES FAILS TO DO THIS, FIGURATIVELY.

Now arrange the circled letters to form the surprise answer, as suggested by the above cartoon.

Print answer here " ◯◯◯◯ THE ◯◯◯◯◯◯◯◯ "

JUMBLE®

Unscramble these four Jumbles, one letter
to each square, to form four ordinary words.

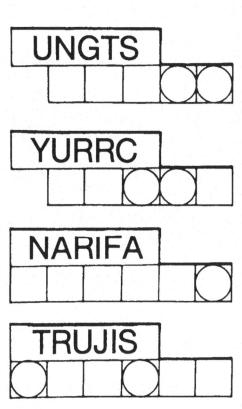

UNGTS

YURRC

NARIFA

TRUJIS

Gee—I'm glad to be out of there

WHAT KIND OF AN
EXPERIENCE WAS IT
FOR THE JINNI TO BE
IN THAT BOTTLE?

Now arrange the circled letters
to form the surprise answer, as
suggested by the above cartoon.

Print answer here A ⬡⬡⬡⬡⬡⬡⬡ ONE

JUMBLE®

Unscramble these four Jumbles, one letter
to each square, to form four ordinary words.

KNALB

AWAMC

BAACAN

TRINWY

I know everyone is
prepared today

I sure
hope so

WHAT THE COLLEGE
HALFBACK WAS IN
HIS STUDIES.

Now arrange the circled letters
to form the surprise answer, as
suggested by the above cartoon.

Print answer here

JUMBLE®

Unscramble these four Jumbles, one letter
to each square, to form four ordinary words.

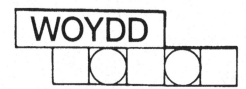

WOYDD

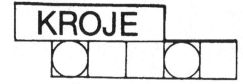

KROJE

SAYMUL

BYTEAU

SHE HAD A STEADY JOB TRYING TO KEEP HIM AT THIS.

Now arrange the circled letters
to form the surprise answer, as
suggested by the above cartoon.

Print answer here   A

45

JUMBLE®

Unscramble these four Jumbles, one letter
to each square, to form four ordinary words.

VUSEA

DAIBE

TINEKT

ROBAHR

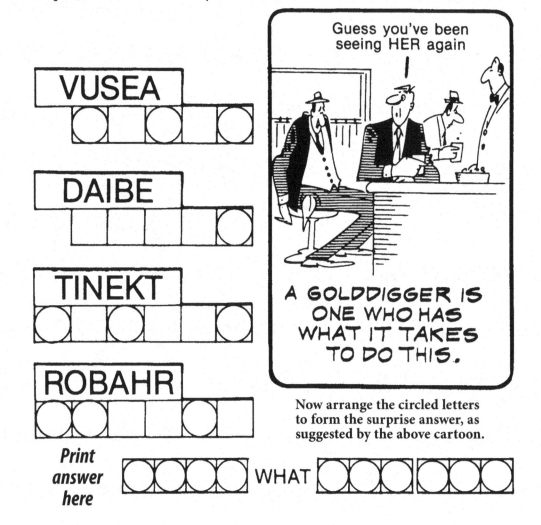

Guess you've been
seeing HER again

A GOLDDIGGER IS
ONE WHO HAS
WHAT IT TAKES
TO DO THIS.

Now arrange the circled letters
to form the surprise answer, as
suggested by the above cartoon.

Print
answer
here

◯◯◯◯ WHAT ◯◯◯◯ ◯◯◯◯

JUMBLE®

Unscramble these four Jumbles, one letter to each square, to form four ordinary words.

OYLED

GYROP

LINKUE

JOBTEC

This looks like a sure thing

Too risky for me

COULD BE A SKEPTIC'S OUTLOOK.

Now arrange the circled letters to form the surprise answer, as suggested by the above cartoon.

Print answer here A " ◯◯◯◯◯◯ ◯◯◯◯ "

JUMBLE®

Unscramble these four Jumbles, one letter
to each square, to form four ordinary words.

BLAYK

DIXEO

BIFCAR

ENPLYT

A BUSINESSMAN IS
JUDGED BY THE
COMPANY HE
KEEPS ---

Now arrange the circled letters
to form the surprise answer, as
suggested by the above cartoon.

Print answer here

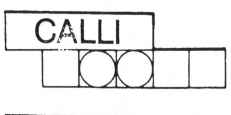

Unscramble these four Jumbles, one letter
to each square, to form four ordinary words.

CALLI

WOPER

TAMENG

RUBENK

THAT BORE WON'T
STOP TALKING UNTIL
YOU START THIS.

Now arrange the circled letters
to form the surprise answer, as
suggested by the above cartoon.

Print answer here

JUMBLE®

Unscramble these four Jumbles, one letter
to each square, to form four ordinary words.

GINOG

BORNI

HUSTYP

PHYNOT

HOW HE USUALLY
ENDED A SENTENCE.

Now arrange the circled letters
to form the surprise answer, as
suggested by the above cartoon.

*Print
answer
here*

WITH
A " "

JUMBLE®

Unscramble these four Jumbles, one letter
to each square, to form four ordinary words.

FRUMO

YOULS

REDAIM

ATJECK

Fits you like
a glove

$

$

WHAT HE GOT
WHEN HE BOUGHT
THAT "STYLISH"
RAINCOAT.

Now arrange the circled letters
to form the surprise answer, as
suggested by the above cartoon.

Print answer here " ◯◯◯◯◯◯◯ "

JUMBLE®

Unscramble these four Jumbles, one letter
to each square, to form four ordinary words.

YAASS

BICCU

RILOAS

FRYTAC

Culture for beginners

WHAT SHE
THOUGHT THAT NEW
FRESHMAN WAS.

Now arrange the circled letters
to form the surprise answer, as
suggested by the above cartoon.

*Print
answer
here* VERY "○○○○○ – ○○○○○"

JUMBLE®

Unscramble these four Jumbles, one letter
to each square, to form four ordinary words.

YOWNS

GEBOF

SMEECH

HIRSLE

Now arrange the circled letters
to form the surprise answer, as
suggested by the above cartoon.

Print answer here

JUMBLE®

Unscramble these four Jumbles, one letter to each square, to form four ordinary words.

MUIBE

LOFAR

SLEAWE

DULBOY

There've been some changes since I was last here

WHAT THOSE NEWLY HATCHED TERMITES WERE.

Now arrange the circled letters to form the surprise answer, as suggested by the above cartoon.

Print answer here

⬡⬡⬡⬡⬡ IN THE ⬡⬡⬡⬡

JUMBLE®

Unscramble these four Jumbles, one letter
to each square, to form four ordinary words.

NOTIX

POAKK

GATHUC

RYMILG

We want our money back

SOMETIMES WHEN THE
PLAYERS DO THE
RUNNING, THE FANS
DO THIS.

Now arrange the circled letters
to form the surprise answer, as
suggested by the above cartoon.

Print answer here THE

JUMBLE®

Unscramble these four Jumbles, one letter to each square, to form four ordinary words.

SASIB

ECTAN

TABBIR

FATOLA

WHAT SOME PARENTS EXPERIENCE WHEN THEY HAVE TEEN-AGE KIDS.

Now arrange the circled letters to form the surprise answer, as suggested by the above cartoon.

Print answer here " _____ "

JUMBLE®

Unscramble these four Jumbles, one letter
to each square, to form four ordinary words.

DYLAL

EVVER

YETHIG

TEENAB

Some
family!

But no worse
than most others

WHAT MANY
FAMILY PROBLEMS
ARE.

Now arrange the circled letters
to form the surprise answer, as
suggested by the above cartoon.

Print answer here ALL "⬡⬡⬡⬡⬡⬡⬡⬡⬡"

JUMBLE®

Unscramble these four Jumbles, one letter
to each square, to form four ordinary words.

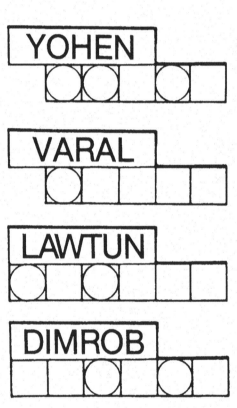

YOHEN

VARAL

LAWTUN

DIMROB

IF HE STARTS RIGHT
OUT COMPLAINING
ABOUT HER COOKING,
SHE'LL LEARN
BETTER---

Now arrange the circled letters
to form the surprise answer, as
suggested by the above cartoon.

Print answer here

JUMBLE

Unscramble these four Jumbles, one letter to each square, to form four ordinary words.

YIEPT

DRIAP

PADIUN

TULYSS

HOW MANY A "CHECKERED" CAREER ENDS UP.

Now arrange the circled letters to form the surprise answer, as suggested by the above cartoon.

Print answer here

IN A

JUMBLE®

Unscramble these four Jumbles, one letter
to each square, to form four ordinary words.

RUYLS

NYPOH

STYJUL

TRALFE

Wonder how
he makes
his living

A lot of
people found
out--to their
sorrow

ANY MAN WHO
SURVIVES BY "DOING
NOTHING" IS PROBABLY
REALLY DOING THIS.

Now arrange the circled letters
to form the surprise answer, as
suggested by the above cartoon.

Print answer here

JUMBLE®

Unscramble these four Jumbles, one letter
to each square, to form four ordinary words.

TRAAL

SOITH

FRYLUR

EPALUG

WHY HE WAS SO
POPULAR IN JAIL.

Now arrange the circled letters
to form the surprise answer, as
suggested by the above cartoon.

Print answer here

HE WAS "☐☐☐☐☐☐" OF THE ☐☐☐☐☐☐

JUMBLE®

Unscramble these four Jumbles, one letter
to each square, to form four ordinary words.

DUXEE

CARPH

LARCOR

NARFIA

AN OUTFIT THAT
MAKES ONE WOMAN
LOOK SLIM OFTEN
MAKES OTHERS
LOOK THIS.

Now arrange the circled letters
to form the surprise answer, as
suggested by the above cartoon.

Print answer here " _____ "

JUMBLE®

Unscramble these four Jumbles, one letter to each square, to form four ordinary words.

ASTEE

LAHCK

SCEXIE

REDDEG

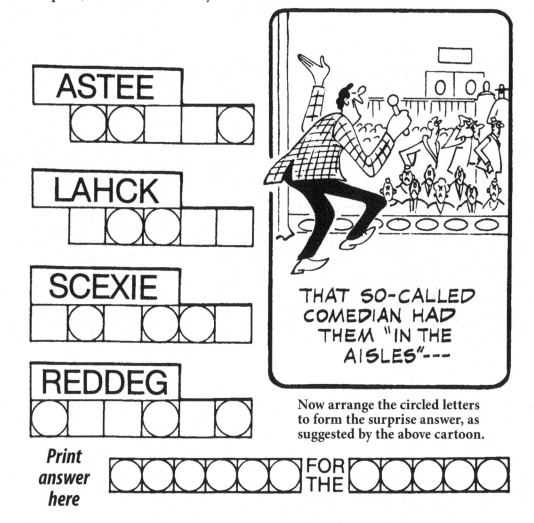

THAT SO-CALLED COMEDIAN HAD THEM "IN THE AISLES"---

Now arrange the circled letters to form the surprise answer, as suggested by the above cartoon.

Print answer here

☐☐☐☐☐☐ FOR THE ☐☐☐☐☐

JUMBLE®

Unscramble these four Jumbles, one letter
to each square, to form four ordinary words.

HYSYL

REDEL

FLEMUF

THORAU

THEY SAID SHE WAS
BEAUTIFUL BUT
NOT QUITE THIS.

Now arrange the circled letters
to form the surprise answer, as
suggested by the above cartoon.

Print answer here " ◯◯◯ ◯◯◯◯◯ "

JUMBLE®

Unscramble these four Jumbles, one letter
to each square, to form four ordinary words.

NIKKY

MAGLE

SVALIE

LAIWHE

He shouldn't be
gossiping like that

ONE WAY TO KEEP
FRIENDS IS NOT
TO DO THIS.

Now arrange the circled letters
to form the surprise answer, as
suggested by the above cartoon.

Print answer
here "⬭⬭⬭⬭⬭ THEM ⬭⬭⬭⬭"

JUMBLE®

Unscramble these four Jumbles, one letter
to each square, to form four ordinary words.

TASID
◯ ◯ ◯ ◯ ◯ ◯

KOPER
◯ ◯ ◯ ◯ ◯

FLENNE
◯ ◯ ◯ ◯ ◯ ◯

POATTE
◯ ◯ ◯ ◯ ◯ ◯

PEOPLE WHO TRAVEL
IN ORDER TO
BECOME BROADENED
SOMETIMES RETURN
HOME THIS WAY.

Now arrange the circled letters
to form the surprise answer, as
suggested by the above cartoon.

Print answer here " ◯◯◯◯◯◯◯◯◯◯ "

JUMBLE®

Unscramble these four Jumbles, one letter
to each square, to form four ordinary words.

SUPIO

TRONS

GANTOU

FEINED

What kinda
eats you
got?

Knock it off--
this ain't one
of your greasy
spoons

WHAT COULD BE
MORE ELEGANT THAN
"EATING OUT"?

Now arrange the circled letters
to form the surprise answer, as
suggested by the above cartoon.

Print answer here " ◯◯◯◯◯◯ ◯◯◯ "

JUMBLE®

Unscramble these four Jumbles, one letter to each square, to form four ordinary words.

USTIE

TARIE

RIDAFA

INGLEM

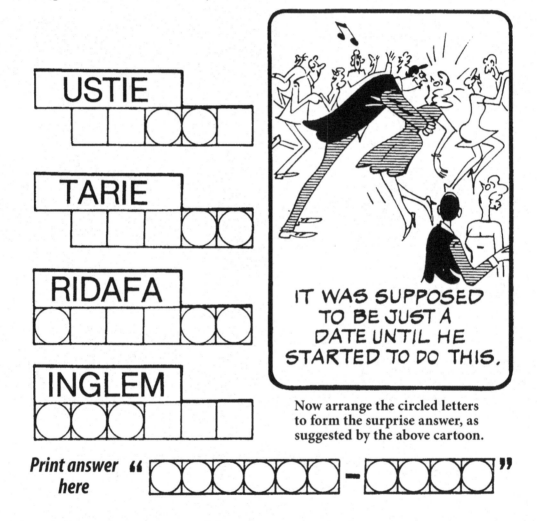

IT WAS SUPPOSED TO BE JUST A DATE UNTIL HE STARTED TO DO THIS.

Now arrange the circled letters to form the surprise answer, as suggested by the above cartoon.

Print answer here "◯◯◯◯◯◯ – ◯◯◯◯"

JUMBLE®

Unscramble these four Jumbles, one letter
to each square, to form four ordinary words.

VELOR

STACE

REDONP

NAHMLY

He knew
the
secret
of
success

OUR
FOUNDER

TO ACHIEVE A
"TRIUMPH" IN LIFE,
ONE MUST PUT
THESE TOGETHER
IN COMBINATION.

Now arrange the circled letters
to form the surprise answer, as
suggested by the above cartoon.

Print
answer
here

A " ☐☐☐ " & PLENTY " ☐☐☐☐☐ "
OF

JUMBLE®

Unscramble these four Jumbles, one letter to each square, to form four ordinary words.

YORFE

SPUHL

VAHLIS

NARBER

WHAT HE CLAIMED HE GAVE HIS WIFE.

Now arrange the circled letters to form the surprise answer, as suggested by the above cartoon.

Print answer here

THE BEST "◯◯◯◯" OF HIS ◯◯◯◯

JUMBLE®

Unscramble these four Jumbles, one letter to each square, to form four ordinary words.

NOCIT

TONJI

PAICEE

RISDAM

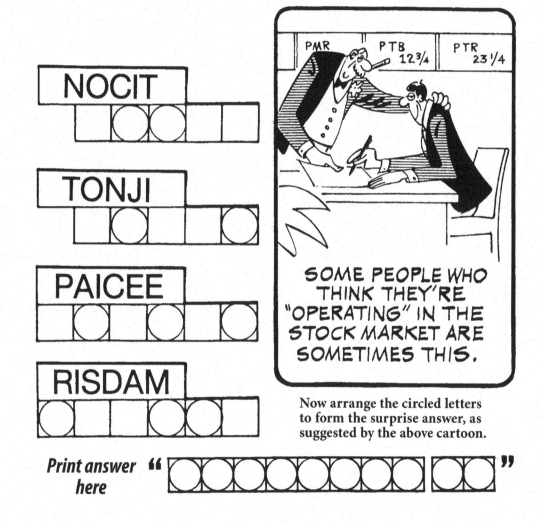

PMR   PTB 12¾   PTR 23¼

SOME PEOPLE WHO THINK THEY'RE "OPERATING" IN THE STOCK MARKET ARE SOMETIMES THIS.

Now arrange the circled letters to form the surprise answer, as suggested by the above cartoon.

Print answer here " ◯◯◯◯◯◯◯◯ ◯◯ "

JUMBLE®

Unscramble these four Jumbles, one letter
to each square, to form four ordinary words.

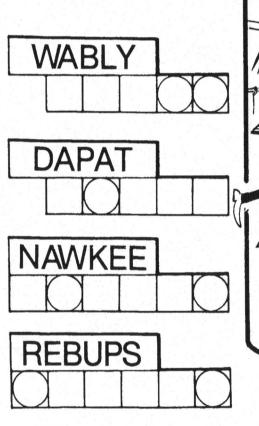

WABLY

DAPAT

NAWKEE

REBUPS

Stocks went down and it
looks like rain

THE PESSIMIST HAD
A HAPPY LOOK EVERY
TIME HE HAD THIS
TO REPORT.

Now arrange the circled letters
to form the surprise answer, as
suggested by the above cartoon.

Print answer here

JUMBLE®

Unscramble these four Jumbles, one letter
to each square, to form four ordinary words.

TAHBE

GYTIN

BROTED

DERAIM

You mean you've NEVER
been married?

WHAT SHE HAD
WHEN SHE MET
THAT ELIGIBLE
YOUNG BACHELOR.

Now arrange the circled letters
to form the surprise answer, as
suggested by the above cartoon.

Print answer
here   A "⬡⬡⬡⬡⬡⬡" ⬡⬡⬡⬡

JUMBLE®

Unscramble these four Jumbles, one letter
to each square, to form four ordinary words.

FRYOT

RUSUP

UNMIFF

HUNGOE

Lemme give you MY views on that

SOME PEOPLE
APPROACH EVERY
SUBJECT WITH THIS.

Now arrange the circled letters
to form the surprise answer, as
suggested by the above cartoon.

Print answer here   AN ◯◯◯◯◯ ◯◯◯◯◯

JUMBLE®

Unscramble these four Jumbles, one letter
to each square, to form four ordinary words.

CHURS

LAMBY

TENNIA

HOARIM

Better snap
it up

This'll just
take a sec

YOU'RE EXPECTED
TO MAKE IT
IN A HURRY.

Now arrange the circled letters
to form the surprise answer, as
suggested by the above cartoon.

Print answer here

JUMBLE®

Unscramble these four Jumbles, one letter to each square, to form four ordinary words.

TUCEA

RAWEY

FLOUJY

DINKLY

All that money and he gets no fun out of life

ALL WORK AND NO PLAY MAKES THIS.

Now arrange the circled letters to form the surprise answer, as suggested by the above cartoon.

Print answer here "☐☐☐☐" THE ☐☐☐☐ ☐☐☐

JUMBLE®

Unscramble these four Jumbles, one letter to each square, to form four ordinary words.

NOFEL

BREWO

SURWAL

KORSEM

Ask me anything-- I'm a walking encyclopedia

Doesn't know as much as he thinks he does

A WISE MAN NEVER DOES THIS.

Now arrange the circled letters to form the surprise answer, as suggested by the above cartoon.

Print answer here

HIS " "

JUMBLE®

Unscramble these four Jumbles, one letter
to each square, to form four ordinary words.

DICHE

ALLIC

YUTPED

VIRQUE

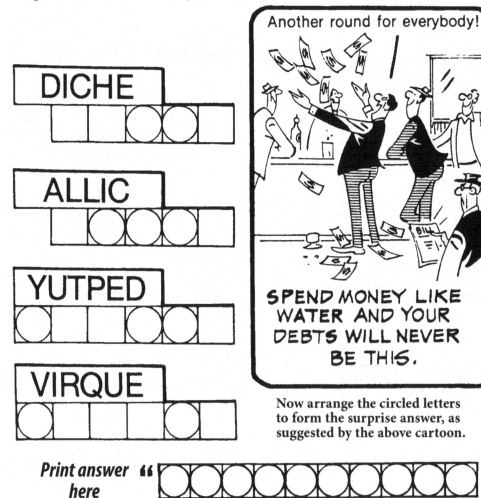

Another round for everybody!

SPEND MONEY LIKE
WATER AND YOUR
DEBTS WILL NEVER
BE THIS.

Now arrange the circled letters
to form the surprise answer, as
suggested by the above cartoon.

Print answer " ◯◯◯◯◯◯◯◯◯◯◯◯ "
here

JUMBLE®

Unscramble these four Jumbles, one letter to each square, to form four ordinary words.

BUNGE

CAPHO

JOACLE

EISORE

TOWN CENTER WASHOUT

LOVERS LANE

WHAT A FORK IN THE ROAD MIGHT HAVE RESULTED IN WAY BACK IN THOSE DAYS.

Now arrange the circled letters to form the surprise answer, as suggested by the above cartoon.

Print answer here

A " ◯◯◯◯◯ " IN THE ◯◯◯

JUMBLE®

Unscramble these four Jumbles, one letter to each square, to form four ordinary words.

NAWGO

IMODI

DELUVA

SNAMEA

WHY SOME HUSBANDS THINK ABOUT RUNNING AWAY TO BECOME OUTLAWS.

Now arrange the circled letters to form the surprise answer, as suggested by the above cartoon.

Print answer here   TO ◯◯◯◯◯ ◯◯ – ◯◯◯◯

JUMBLE®

Unscramble these four Jumbles, one letter
to each square, to form four ordinary words.

GHUDO
◯ ◯ ◯ ◯ ◯

PRIGE
◯ ◯ ◯ ◯ ◯

MUCPIE
◯ ◯ ◯ ◯ ◯ ◯

LAWHER
◯ ◯ ◯ ◯ ◯ ◯

THEY USED TO CALL
HIM THE CREAM
OF FIGHTERS—UNTIL
HE GOT THIS.

Now arrange the circled letters
to form the surprise answer, as
suggested by the above cartoon.

Print answer here " ◯ ◯ ◯ ◯ ◯ ◯ ◯ ◯ "

JUMBLE®

Unscramble these four Jumbles, one letter
to each square, to form four ordinary words.

WETHA

LAIDY

GUYSAR

NIRGIF

THE HORSE YOU
PUT YOUR MONEY
ON OFTEN
DOES THIS.

Now arrange the circled letters
to form the surprise answer, as
suggested by the above cartoon.

Print answer
here ◯◯◯◯ ◯◯◯◯ WITH ◯◯

JUMBLE®

Unscramble these four Jumbles, one letter to each square, to form four ordinary words.

HAABS

THANC

YAMSIL

LOFUND

A STUBBORN MAN DOESN'T HOLD OPINIONS---

Now arrange the circled letters to form the surprise answer, as suggested by the above cartoon.

Print answer here THEY ⬡⬡⬡⬡ ⬡⬡⬡

JUMBLE®

Unscramble these four Jumbles, one letter
to each square, to form four ordinary words.

ZIMEA

LAVIE

VARQUE

FATSIE

Good old Cousin Elmer sure
struck it big

IN ADDITION TO
MONEY, THE RICH
NEVER SEEM TO
LACK THIS.

Now arrange the circled letters
to form the surprise answer, as
suggested by the above cartoon.

**Print answer
here** **Print answer here**

JUMBLE®

Unscramble these four Jumbles, one letter
to each square, to form four ordinary words.

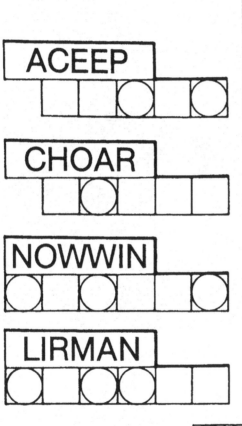

ACEEP
☐☐◯☐◯

CHOAR
☐◯☐☐☐

NOWWIN
◯☐◯☐☐◯

LIRMAN
◯☐◯☐◯☐

There's work to be done
out there, dear

THEY USED TO
CONSIDER HIM A
"RAKE," BUT NOW
HE'S SIMPLY
TURNED INTO THIS.

Now arrange the circled letters
to form the surprise answer, as
suggested by the above cartoon.

Print answer here A ◯◯◯◯◯ ◯◯◯◯◯

JUMBLE®

Unscramble these four Jumbles, one letter to each square, to form four ordinary words.

CHATY

YURMK

KLUNIE

GOFERR

HE BUILT A GOOD FIRE, AND SHE SAID THIS.

Now arrange the circled letters to form the surprise answer, as suggested by the above cartoon.

Print answer here
Print answer here

" ☐☐☐☐☐☐ – ☐☐☐ ! "

JUMBLE®

Unscramble these four Jumbles, one letter to each square, to form four ordinary words.

VENOW

HAKSY

TOOCLE

HOPOUK

Wasn't fast enough with those punches

THE BOXING RING IS NO PLACE FOR THIS.

Now arrange the circled letters to form the surprise answer, as suggested by the above cartoon.

Print answer here A ⬡⬡⬡⬡⬡ " ⬡⬡⬡⬡ "

JUMBLE®

Unscramble these four Jumbles, one letter to each square, to form four ordinary words.

CYDEA

NEQUE

DRIFOL

LIERIX

Uh, oh... I'd better scram

WHAT THE STAG DID WHEN THE HUNTERS ARRIVED.

Now arrange the circled letters to form the surprise answer, as suggested by the above cartoon.

Print answer here

◯◯◯ FOR "◯◯◯◯◯" ◯◯◯◯◯

JUMBLE®

Unscramble these four Jumbles, one letter to each square, to form four ordinary words.

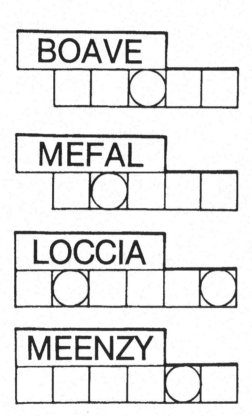

BOAVE

MEFAL

LOCCIA

MEENZY

WHAT THE BIG DAIRY FARMER HAD LOTS OF.

Now arrange the circled letters to form the surprise answer, as suggested by the above cartoon.

Print answer here " ◯◯◯ – ◯◯ "

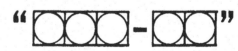

JUMBLE®

Unscramble these four Jumbles, one letter
to each square, to form four ordinary words.

WYDDO

TALUF

BOLLAG

PINSOO

WHAT SHE PROCEEDED
TO DO AFTER HER
BOYFRIEND CANCELED
THEIR DATE.

Now arrange the circled letters
to form the surprise answer, as
suggested by the above cartoon.

Print answer here ⬡⬡⬡⬡ HER ⬡⬡⬡

JUMBLE ®

Unscramble these four Jumbles, one letter
to each square, to form four ordinary words.

MICER

ORFEC

PREDIM

NAILET

Have another one on the house

HE'S SUPPOSED TO
BE WORKING AT THE
DOCK FOR PAY, BUT
HE PREFERS TO
DO THIS.

Now arrange the circled letters
to form the surprise answer, as
suggested by the above cartoon.

Print answer here "◯◯◯◯◯" ◯◯◯◯

JUMBLE®

Unscramble these four Jumbles, one letter to each square, to form four ordinary words.

DRYIT

REQUE

MELVUL

STENOX

WHY HIS CONSCIENCE WAS CLEAN.

Now arrange the circled letters to form the surprise answer, as suggested by the above cartoon.

Print answer here HE ◯◯◯◯◯ ◯◯◯◯ IT

JUMBLE®

Unscramble these four Jumbles, one letter to each square, to form four ordinary words.

ZYZUF

NAUHM

LAVOAW

DOSPYR

This isn't easy

WHAT THAT BUFFET DINNER WAS SORT OF.

Now arrange the circled letters to form the surprise answer, as suggested by the above cartoon.

Print answer here " ⬡⬡⬡ – ⬡⬡⬡⬡⬡⬡ "

JUMBLE®

Unscramble these four Jumbles, one letter
to each square, to form four ordinary words.

THILG

WALOG

BOBING

ENNOIT

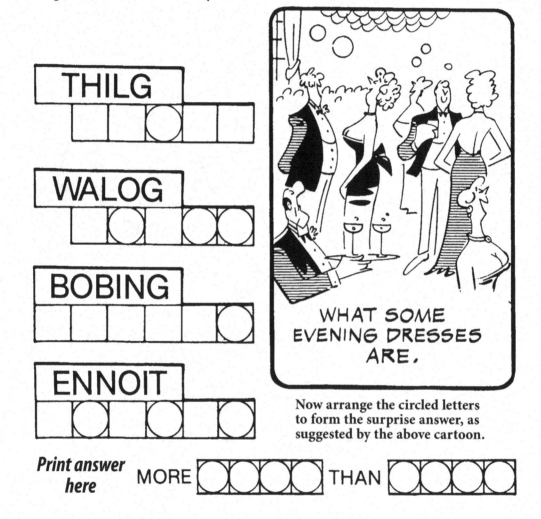

WHAT SOME
EVENING DRESSES
ARE.

Now arrange the circled letters
to form the surprise answer, as
suggested by the above cartoon.

**Print answer
here**   MORE ⬡⬡⬡⬡⬡ THAN ⬡⬡⬡⬡

JUMBLE®

Unscramble these four Jumbles, one letter to each square, to form four ordinary words.

FINKE
○○○□□

NILTE
□□○○○

BAUSCA
□□○○□○

ROTGOT
○○□□□○□

WHERE THE FANATIC'S TRAIN OF THOUGHT ALWAYS RAN.

Now arrange the circled letters to form the surprise answer, as suggested by the above cartoon.

Print answer here

ON A ○○○○○○ ○○○○○

JUMBLE®

Unscramble these four Jumbles, one letter
to each square, to form four ordinary words.

ICCUB

CINEW

YINTTE

GANDEA

There were some bargains I
just couldn't resist

HER PROMISE TO
BE ON TIME
CARRIED A LOT
OF THIS.

Now arrange the circled letters
to form the surprise answer, as
suggested by the above cartoon.

Print answer here " ◯◯◯◯ "

JUMBLE®

Unscramble these four Jumbles, one letter
to each square, to form four ordinary words.

PULIT

TINAF

CRIMET

GLAITH

My dear--you look divine

But you could lose a few pounds

SOME PEOPLE ARE TACTFUL, WHILE OTHERS DO THIS.

Now arrange the circled letters
to form the surprise answer, as
suggested by the above cartoon.

Print answer here ⟨◯◯◯◯◯⟩ THE ⟨◯◯◯◯◯⟩

JUMBLE®

Unscramble these four Jumbles, one letter to each square, to form four ordinary words.

NAGLD

YOGUN

TENTAX

ROCCEE

But they're getting golden parachutes

WHAT HAPPENED TO THOSE EXECUTIVES WHEN THERE WAS A TAKEOVER AT THE FOOD-PROCESSING COMPANY.

Now arrange the circled letters to form the surprise answer, as suggested by the above cartoon.

Print answer here THEY " "

JUMBLE®

Unscramble these four Jumbles, one letter to each square, to form four ordinary words.

NOWRC

ENKLE

INCLAG

FACSIO

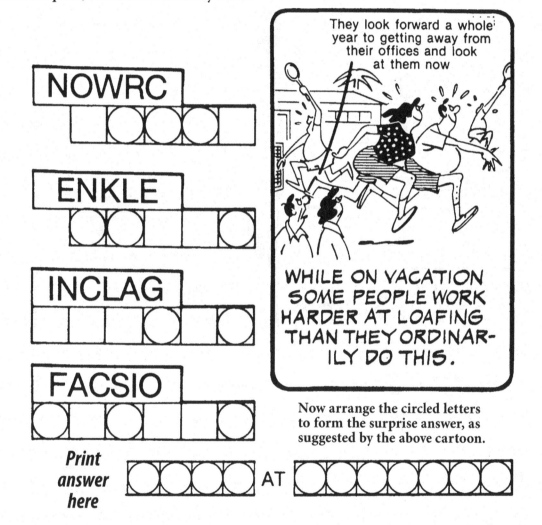

They look forward a whole year to getting away from their offices and look at them now

WHILE ON VACATION SOME PEOPLE WORK HARDER AT LOAFING THAN THEY ORDINAR-ILY DO THIS.

Now arrange the circled letters to form the surprise answer, as suggested by the above cartoon.

Print answer here

☐☐☐☐ AT ☐☐☐☐☐☐☐☐

JUMBLE®

Unscramble these four Jumbles, one letter
to each square, to form four ordinary words.

TIXYS

MERIN

VERPOL

CUTLED

A MAN USUALLY
CAN'T THINK
STRAIGHT WHEN HE
ONLY HAS THIS.

Now arrange the circled letters
to form the surprise answer, as
suggested by the above cartoon.

Print answer here ◯◯◯◯◯◯ ON HIS ◯◯◯◯

JUMBLE®

Unscramble these four Jumbles, one letter
to each square, to form four ordinary words.

SYSUF

HAGUL

LUBBEA

MILTEG

HE WHO
INDULGES---

Now arrange the circled letters
to form the surprise answer, as
suggested by the above cartoon.

Print answer here

JUMBLE®

Unscramble these four Jumbles, one letter to each square, to form four ordinary words.

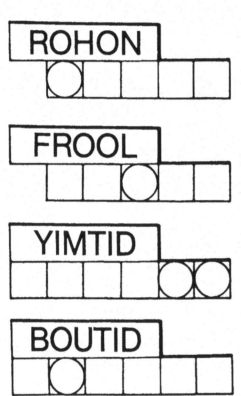

ROHON

FROOL

YIMTID

BOUTID

THIS MIGHT BE MORE APPRECIATED IF WE WERE GIVEN IT LATER IN LIFE.

Now arrange the circled letters to form the surprise answer, as suggested by the above cartoon.

Print answer here

JUMBLE®

Unscramble these four Jumbles, one letter
to each square, to form four ordinary words.

LIDLR

VABEO

DREEMY

GORNDA

We have another raise from number six.

You're not getting this one, Louise.

6

Back off, Tina!

2

PRICES AT THE AUCTION WERE GOING UP AND UP. THIS WOULD GO ON UNTIL THE ---

Now arrange the circled letters
to form the surprise answer, as
suggested by the above cartoon.

Print
answer
here

" ◯◯◯◯◯◯ " ◯◯◯

JUMBLE®

Unscramble these four Jumbles, one letter to each square, to form four ordinary words.

NADKR

PILEM

UNYIMT

YGLEAL

The Pine Tree State is almost as large as all the other New England states combined.

Wow!

THE LARGEST NEW ENGLAND STATE HAS 3,478 MILES OF COASTLINE BORDERING THE ---

Now arrange the circled letters to form the surprise answer, as suggested by the above cartoon.

Print answer here " ☐☐☐☐☐☐ - ☐☐☐☐ "

JUMBLE®

Unscramble these four Jumbles, one letter
to each square, to form four ordinary words.

UDLEE

HENSE

VEEMRO

FIROPT

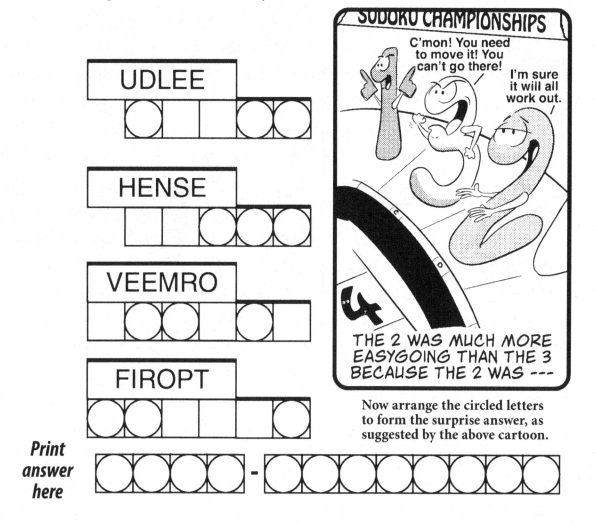

SUDOKU CHAMPIONSHIPS

C'mon! You need
to move it! You
can't go there!

I'm sure
it will all
work out.

4

THE 2 WAS MUCH MORE
EASYGOING THAN THE 3
BECAUSE THE 2 WAS ---

Now arrange the circled letters
to form the surprise answer, as
suggested by the above cartoon.

**Print
answer
here**

◯◯◯◯ - ◯◯◯◯◯◯◯◯◯

JUMBLE®

Unscramble these four Jumbles, one letter to each square, to form four ordinary words.

TIKYT

INAPO

LFENUN

NADETL

It's "The Adventures of Robin Hood." Errol has signed on. What do you say?

Of course I want to do it! I love Errol!

OLIVIA DE HAVILLAND WOULD PLAY MAID MARIAN TO ERROL'S ROBIN HOOD. SHE WAS ---

Now arrange the circled letters to form the surprise answer, as suggested by the above cartoon.

Print answer here

JUMBLE®

Unscramble these four Jumbles, one letter
to each square, to form four ordinary words.

SCEHS

KROPE

GHEYUL

SNSITI

These seats were
expensive, but
they were so
worth it.

I'll
say!

THE WEALTHY COUPLE
ALWAYS FLEW FIRST
CLASS AND COULD
WELL AFFORD ---

Now arrange the circled letters
to form the surprise answer, as
suggested by the above cartoon.

Print
answer
here

⬡⬡⬡-⬡⬡⬡⬡⬡   ⬡⬡⬡⬡⬡⬡

JUMBLE®

Unscramble these four Jumbles, one letter to each square, to form four ordinary words.

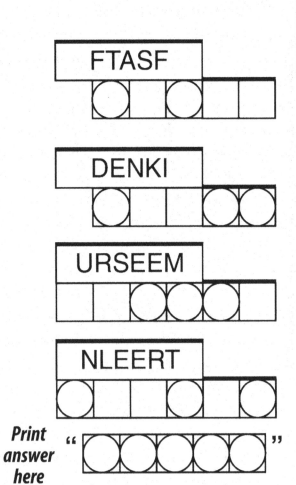

FTASF

DENKI

URSEEM

NLEERT

This is wonderful. I think we're all going to sleep well tonight.

I'm ready to hit that beautiful bed.

AFTER UPGRADING TO LODGING WITH TWO BEDROOMS, THEY WOULD HAVE ---

Now arrange the circled letters to form the surprise answer, as suggested by the above cartoon.

Print answer here " ◯◯◯◯◯ " ◯◯◯◯◯◯

JUMBLE®

Unscramble these four Jumbles, one letter
to each square, to form four ordinary words.

MHEET

LLSYY

PLUTIP

JURNIE

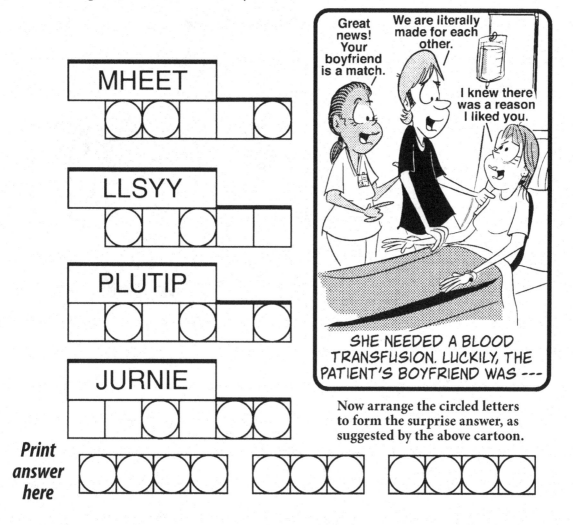

Great
news!
Your
boyfriend
is a match.

We are literally
made for each
other.

I knew there
was a reason
I liked you.

SHE NEEDED A BLOOD
TRANSFUSION. LUCKILY, THE
PATIENT'S BOYFRIEND WAS ---

Now arrange the circled letters
to form the surprise answer, as
suggested by the above cartoon.

Print
answer
here

JUMBLE®

Unscramble these four Jumbles, one letter
to each square, to form four ordinary words.

UGGEO

PGUYP

ONEDOL

SSUHAQ

You know,
you could
rent a tilling
machine.

Are you
kidding me?
I love doing
this.

WHEN IT CAME TO
TILLING THE SOIL BY
HAND, HE WAS ---

Now arrange the circled letters
to form the surprise answer, as
suggested by the above cartoon.

Print answer here ◯◯◯◯ " ◯◯◯ "

JUMBLE®

Unscramble these four Jumbles, one letter
to each square, to form four ordinary words.

UKAQE

PNIYP

ZALLYI

LOBUED

So, which is it, A or B?

I don't know. I'm not good at tests.

I'm going with B.

A   B

FIZZY FUN
TASTE TES

THE BLIND TASTE TEST
BETWEEN THE COLA
BRANDS WAS A ---

Now arrange the circled letters
to form the surprise answer, as
suggested by the above cartoon.

Print answer here ◯◯◯ ◯◯◯◯

JUMBLE

Unscramble these four Jumbles, one letter
to each square, to form four ordinary words.

SUBTR

FMEAR

LENFAL

MLOGOY

I threw it
as hard as
I could.

Wow!
You're
way
short.

THE "HOLES" ON
THE FRISBEE GOLF
COURSE WERE ---

Now arrange the circled letters
to form the surprise answer, as
suggested by the above cartoon.

Print answer here ◯◯◯ - ◯◯◯◯◯

112

JUMBLE®

Unscramble these four Jumbles, one letter
to each square, to form four ordinary words.

GULHA

TUYNT

OCYNOL

RYNEFZ

We need to modernize this. Get rid of it.

Right away, Your Majesty.

THE KING HATED HIS CHAIR
AND WANTED IT TO BE ---

Now arrange the circled letters
to form the surprise answer, as
suggested by the above cartoon.

Print
answer
here

" ◯◯◯◯◯◯ " ◯◯◯

JUMBLE®

Unscramble these four Jumbles, one letter
to each square, to form four ordinary words.

TMUBH

ZUGEA

CEANCT

SLYMEF

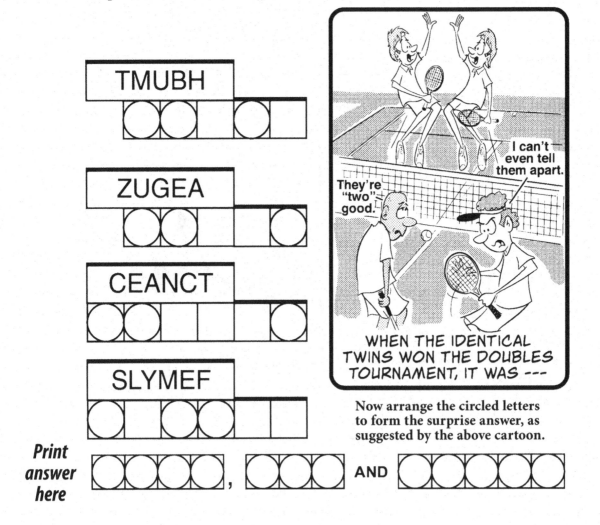

I can't even tell them apart.

They're "two" good.

WHEN THE IDENTICAL
TWINS WON THE DOUBLES
TOURNAMENT, IT WAS ---

Now arrange the circled letters
to form the surprise answer, as
suggested by the above cartoon.

Print
answer
here

⬡⬡⬡⬡ , ⬡⬡⬡ AND ⬡⬡⬡⬡⬡

JUMBLE®

Unscramble these four Jumbles, one letter
to each square, to form four ordinary words.

RUFMO

RADLW

LACCEN

VAROYS

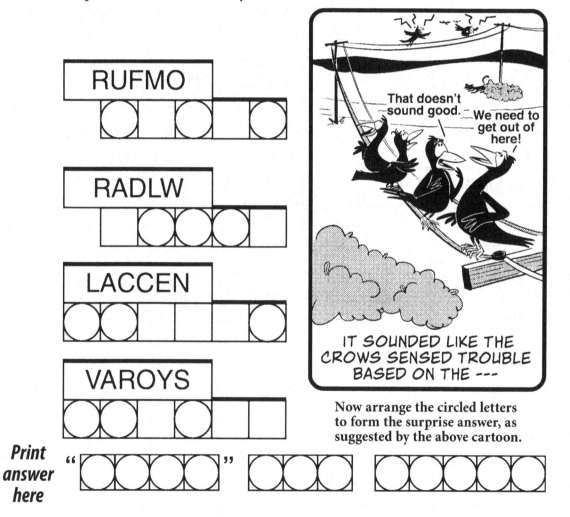

That doesn't sound good.

We need to get out of here!

IT SOUNDED LIKE THE
CROWS SENSED TROUBLE
BASED ON THE ---

Now arrange the circled letters
to form the surprise answer, as
suggested by the above cartoon.

Print answer here

" ⬡⬡⬡⬡⬡ " ⬡⬡⬡ ⬡⬡⬡⬡⬡⬡

JUMBLE®

Unscramble these four Jumbles, one letter to each square, to form four ordinary words.

THONC

AMOMC

WARELY

DINADC

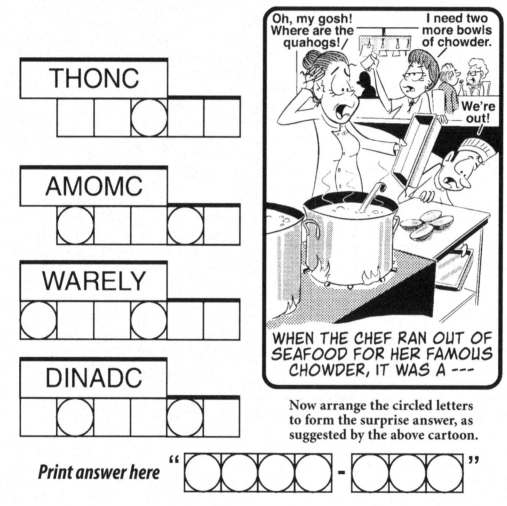

Oh, my gosh! Where are the quahogs!

I need two more bowls of chowder.

We're out!

WHEN THE CHEF RAN OUT OF SEAFOOD FOR HER FAMOUS CHOWDER, IT WAS A ---

Now arrange the circled letters to form the surprise answer, as suggested by the above cartoon.

Print answer here "⬡⬡⬡⬡⬡ - ⬡⬡⬡"

JUMBLE®

Unscramble these four Jumbles, one letter
to each square, to form four ordinary words.

BROOT

LIVTA

AYRSLA

EEFLNN

Who can give
me more
examples?

GIVE
ACCEPT
OBEY
UNTIE
RUN
JUMP

How about,
"talk"?

Throw!

HOW DO YOU SAY ACTION
WORDS SUCH AS GIVE,
ACCEPT, OBEY AND UNTIE?

Now arrange the circled letters
to form the surprise answer, as
suggested by the above cartoon.

Print answer here

JUMBLE®

Unscramble these four Jumbles, one letter
to each square, to form four ordinary words.

ELCTF

PRNUS

GLEYCR

IWIGRN

Thank you for coming.
You are the select few
that I trust.

THE SMALL MEETING
OF THE SHAPES WAS
CALLED BY THE ---

Now arrange the circled letters
to form the surprise answer, as
suggested by the above cartoon.

*Print
answer
here*

JUMBLE®

Unscramble these four Jumbles, one letter to each square, to form four ordinary words.

ODPOR

LXIEE

SKCITY

CLAHNB

Still love that smell, huh?

It's so rich.

THE PENNIES WERE JUST MINTED AND HAD A UNIQUE SMELL. THIS MADE THEM ---

Now arrange the circled letters to form the surprise answer, as suggested by the above cartoon.

Print answer here " ◯◯◯◯◯◯◯ "

JUMBLE®

Unscramble these four Jumbles, one letter
to each square, to form four ordinary words.

HITTG

HNIKT

XUFOOT

NLEENK

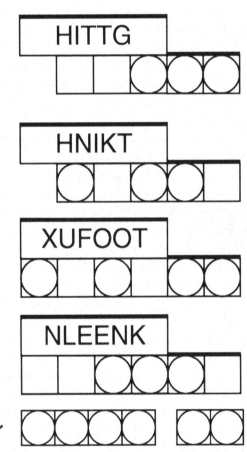

If you have 1, you have a
single thing. If you have 0,
then you don't have any.

012345678

I had zero ice cream
last night.

THE NUMBER 1 IS SO LOW
THAT ITS VALUE IS ---

Now arrange the circled letters
to form the surprise answer, as
suggested by the above cartoon.

Print
answer
here

JUMBLE®

Unscramble these four Jumbles, one letter
to each square, to form four ordinary words.

MYOCF

LEYAM

ENLHIA

LIREOO

Print answer here " ◯◯◯◯ "

It's great to have the kids helping.

I'm done with my room!

I'll dig the kitchen.

Quit whacking me!

WHEN MAKING A NEW HOME, PRAIRIE DOGS BURROW WITH HELP FROM THE ---

Now arrange the circled letters
to form the surprise answer, as
suggested by the above cartoon.

◯◯◯◯◯◯

121

JUMBLE®

Unscramble these four Jumbles, one letter to each square, to form four ordinary words.

TIGZL

LIGRL

NHETCR

TALTET

Changing from a four-way stop will help relieve congestion.

I think we'll all agree to do this.

THEY WANTED TO INSTALL A NEW TRAFFIC SIGNAL AND JUST NEEDED THE CITY TO ---

Now arrange the circled letters to form the surprise answer, as suggested by the above cartoon.

Print answer here

JUMBLE®

Unscramble these four Jumbles, one letter
to each square, to form four ordinary words.

MOSPT

LIVAT

DEWAOM

BLOHEB

Is it true you can
run 55 kilometers
per hour?

Oops! I'm late.
I guess you'll
find out.

THE LARGER MEMBER OF THE
DEER FAMILY HUNG OUT WITH
HIS COUSINS UNTIL HE ---

Now arrange the circled letters
to form the surprise answer, as
suggested by the above cartoon.

**Print
answer
here**

" " "-"

JUMBLE®

Unscramble these four Jumbles, one letter to each square, to form four ordinary words.

ANHEV

FYTAT

DLIYWL

NILFUS

The earth is like a pancake! It's not a sphere!

Is the moon a pancake too? You're making me hungry.

What a nut!

SPEAKERS' CORNER

SOME PEOPLE DON'T BELIEVE THE EARTH IS SPHERICAL AND ---

Now arrange the circled letters to form the surprise answer, as suggested by the above cartoon.

Print answer here

JUMBLE®

Unscramble these four Jumbles, one letter
to each square, to form four ordinary words.

NEIMC

OSTUC

ENAWOP

NAMEHU

How soon did they say the clock was going to be ready?

The last email said they would let us know when it was finished.

THE NEW CLOCK
THEY ORDERED
WOULD BE DELIVERED
AND INSTALLED ---

Now arrange the circled letters
to form the surprise answer, as
suggested by the above cartoon.

Print
answer
here
⎕⎕⎕⎕⎕ THE ⎕⎕⎕⎕⎕ ⎕⎕⎕⎕⎕⎕

JUMBLE.

Unscramble these four Jumbles, one letter to each square, to form four ordinary words.

UQATO

RACYR

UMDIET

LONPEL

I'm glad we had some extra time to practice.

Look at that view! It's beautiful here.

THEY ARRIVED AT THE GOLF COURSE EARLY TO USE THE PRACTICE GREEN AND ---

Now arrange the circled letters to form the surprise answer, as suggested by the above cartoon.

Print answer here

JUMBLE®

Unscramble these four Jumbles, one letter to each square, to form four ordinary words.

TUFEL

GHUSR

ENTTAN

GONULE

Please help yourself. We have plenty more.

This fit when we got on board.

I'm done.

THEY ENJOYED THE CRUISE'S ALL-YOU-CAN-EAT BUFFETS ---

Now arrange the circled letters to form the surprise answer, as suggested by the above cartoon.

Print answer here

JUMBLE®

Unscramble these four Jumbles, one letter to each square, to form four ordinary words.

LRIFL
◯◯◯◯◯

CIFHN
◯◯◯◯◯

YOGAVE
◯◯◯◯◯◯

FRONUF
◯◯◯◯◯◯

FINISH

I have the stamina to see this through to the finish line.

Do you think you can win the election?

WHEN THE WINNER OF THE MARATHON GOT INTO POLITICS, HE ---

Now arrange the circled letters to form the surprise answer, as suggested by the above cartoon.

Print answer here

◯◯◯◯ ◯◯◯◯ ◯◯◯◯◯◯◯

JUMBLE®

Unscramble these four Jumbles, one letter to each square, to form four ordinary words.

PNYPI

TNOEK

SALYGS

CAPEAL

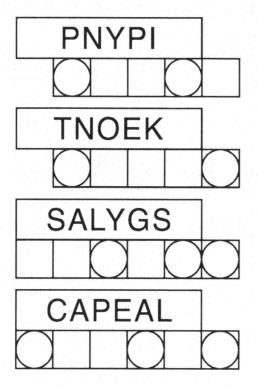

WHEN THE RESTAURANT CHARGED 1 CENT FOR ITS NOODLE DISH, CUSTOMERS ENJOYED THE ---

Now arrange the circled letters to form the surprise answer, as suggested by the above cartoon.

Print answer here "◯◯◯◯◯" ◯◯◯◯◯

JUMBLE®

Unscramble these four Jumbles, one letter to each square, to form four ordinary words.

PUNTI

ESSNE

OMMPPO

CATUPE

OK. Let's go over the protocol one more time.

C'mon, Neil. We're all good. Time for you to make history.

AFTER TOUCHING DOWN ON THE MOON, BUZZ ALDRIN TOLD NEIL ARMSTRONG TO ---

Now arrange the circled letters to form the surprise answer, as suggested by the above cartoon.

Print answer here

JUMBLE®

Unscramble these four Jumbles, one letter
to each square, to form four ordinary words.

LEFTE

OWNOS

DTARSN

CLIEPV

This is going to be risky.
We all need to be brave to pull
this off.

TO ROB FROM THE RICH
AND GIVE TO THE POOR,
ROBIN HOOD NEEDED ---

Now arrange the circled letters
to form the surprise answer, as
suggested by the above cartoon.

*Print
answer
here*

JUMBLE®

Unscramble these four Jumbles, one letter
to each square, to form four ordinary words.

NYIWD

SRIUV

TBEERT

CIDEKW

I can see us
living here.

This will be the perfect
spot for your nest.

Look
down
there.

BUILD
TO SUIT

THEY DECIDED TO BUILD THEIR
NEST NEAR THE SUMMIT
BECAUSE THEY LIKED THE ---

Now arrange the circled letters
to form the surprise answer, as
suggested by the above cartoon.

*Print
answer
here*

◯◯◯◯'◯-◯◯◯ ◯◯◯◯

JUMBLE®

Unscramble these four Jumbles, one letter
to each square, to form four ordinary words.

XYITS

CORFE

WNIMON

RAWTDO

Honey, why are you even trying? Face it, we're both a little bigger.

I know. Oh well.

HE TRIED ON THE PANTS
HE WORE ON HIS WEDDING
DAY, BUT IT WAS A ---

Now arrange the circled letters
to form the surprise answer, as
suggested by the above cartoon.

Print answer here

" ⬡⬡⬡⬡⬡ " ⬡⬡ ⬡⬡⬡⬡

JUMBLE®

Unscramble these four Jumbles, one letter
to each square, to form four ordinary words.

KAIHK

SREDS

ONTINO

SSOOMC

Your online profile said you were an engineer.

I'm a model train engineer. I treat it like my job.

THE COLLECTOR
WHO WOULDN'T STOP
TALKING ABOUT HIS
MODEL TRAIN HAD A ---

Now arrange the circled letters
to form the surprise answer, as
suggested by the above cartoon.

Print
answer
here

◯◯◯-◯◯◯◯◯ ◯◯◯◯

JUMBLE®

Unscramble these four Jumbles, one letter
to each square, to form four ordinary words.

COPOH

DORNF

CITTEK

KANEEW

I thought
you studied.
This is not
acceptable!

I'm
sorry.

Give me your
phone and
turn off the
video games
until you turn
this around.

FAILING HIS HISTORY
TEST WAS A - - -

Now arrange the circled letters
to form the surprise answer, as
suggested by the above cartoon.

Print answer here ◯◯ - " ◯◯◯◯ "

JUMBLE®

Unscramble these four Jumbles, one letter
to each square, to form four ordinary words.

TNNIH

XILPE

REACOS

ROOSUP

AS KIDS OF CAUTIOUS
PARENTS, THEY COULD
ONLY WATCH TV IF THEY
WENT THROUGH THE ---

Now arrange the circled letters
to form the surprise answer, as
suggested by the above cartoon.

*Print
answer
here*

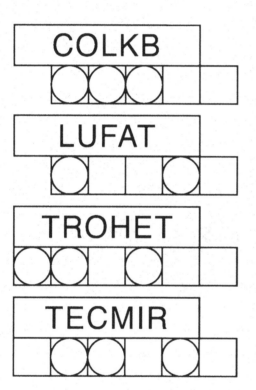

JUMBLE®

Unscramble these four Jumbles, one letter to each square, to form four ordinary words.

COLKB

LUFAT

TROHET

TECMIR

Your new place is amazing! Your waiting room is full. Business must be good.

I have no complaints.

THE PODIATRIST HAD A FANCY NEW OFFICE AND HAD ENOUGH PATIENTS TO ---

Now arrange the circled letters to form the surprise answer, as suggested by the above cartoon.

Print answer here

JUMBLE®

Unscramble these four Jumbles, one letter
to each square, to form four ordinary words.

WOLYL

RAFDU

PORPEC

POSYOK

Make sure people
see my site first
when they search
for a locksmith.

Smith's Locks

"locks" "security"
"safes" "unlock"

I will. So far I have;
"locks", "security",
"safes", "unlock"...

THEY WANTED TO MAKE
SURE THE LOCKSMITH'S NEW
WEBSITE HAD ENOUGH ---

Now arrange the circled letters
to form the surprise answer, as
suggested by the above cartoon.

Print answer here

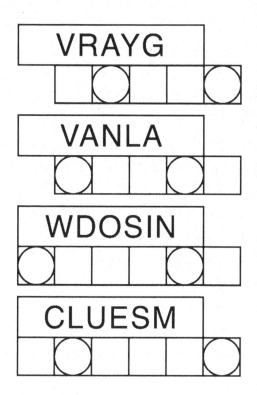

JUMBLE®

Unscramble these four Jumbles, one letter
to each square, to form four ordinary words.

VRAYG

VANLA

WDOSIN

CLUESM

I never thought
they'd start this.

It's a
huge job.

CONSTRUCTION OF THE
SUBWAY TUNNEL WAS ---

Now arrange the circled letters
to form the surprise answer, as
suggested by the above cartoon.

Print answer here

JUMBLE®

Unscramble these four Jumbles, one letter
to each square, to form four ordinary words.

LELYA

TETEH

TYELNG

TREOFG

Wow! It's like I've worn it my whole life.

It's you!

THE HAT MADE OF MATTED
WOOL FIT PERFECTLY AND ---

Now arrange the circled letters
to form the surprise answer, as
suggested by the above cartoon.

**Print answer
here**

JUMBLE®

Unscramble these four Jumbles, one letter
to each square, to form four ordinary words.

GUMLO

SREHF

NINETV

EOMYLD

Hi, Grandpa!

Wow!
You're all
doing great!

Let's hear it for
The Flying
Wallendas.

TIGHTROPE WALKERS
RAN IN HIS FAMILY.
HE CAME FROM A ---

Now arrange the circled letters
to form the surprise answer, as
suggested by the above cartoon.

**Print
answer
here**

JUMBLE®

Unscramble these four Jumbles, one letter
to each square, to form four ordinary words.

VEYNO

GEDDO

PTOSYT

ATLTET

I'll take the usual, one sesame with cream cheese.

My bagels are why you're ranked number one.

PLAIN

POPPY

SESAME

I LOVE BAGELS

THE TENNIS PLAYER'S
FAVORITE BAGEL WAS ---

Now arrange the circled letters
to form the surprise answer, as
suggested by the above cartoon.

Print answer here ◯◯◯-◯◯◯◯◯◯

JUMBLE®

Unscramble these four Jumbles, one letter
to each square, to form four ordinary words.

ZMIOG

OPAYS

SOLMYT

FIXNUL

Wow!
That
stinks.

10,000 years
ago the tar
trapped
these
animals
here.

FOR SOME WOOLY
MAMMOTHS, THE TAR AT
LA BREA IN LOS ANGELES
WAS A ---

Now arrange the circled letters
to form the surprise answer, as
suggested by the above cartoon.

Print answer here

143

JUMBLE®

Unscramble these four Jumbles, one letter
to each square, to form four ordinary words.

FOYLT

RUORB

DBEROT

MOAAEB

They would fill the
trenches with water
as a means of defense.

There was
no getting in
there!

THE TOURISTS ENJOYED
THE VIEW OF THE
CASTLE FROM THE ---

Now arrange the circled letters
to form the surprise answer, as
suggested by the above cartoon.

Print
answer
here

"⬡⬡⬡⬡⬡⬡" ⬡⬡⬡⬡

JUMBLE®

Unscramble these four Jumbles, one letter
to each square, to form four ordinary words.

WETSE

SINBO

SWRNET

NYTARP

THE LAWYER CALLED THE
GRIZZLY TO THE STAND,
SO HE COULD ---

Now arrange the circled letters
to form the surprise answer, as
suggested by the above cartoon.

*Print
answer
here*

JUMBLE®

Unscramble these four Jumbles, one letter to each square, to form four ordinary words.

HMEAS

TYEPT

CNOOHH

MARLOC

Yes! It makes shopping here too convenient.

Don't you live upstairs?

THE FASHION BOUTIQUE BELOW HER APARTMENT WAS ---

Now arrange the circled letters to form the surprise answer, as suggested by the above cartoon.

Print answer here " "

JUMBLE®

Unscramble these four Jumbles, one letter to each square, to form four ordinary words.

TYPT

CKNKO

CARYIP

SANDUI

These are much lighter than I thought they'd be.

GODZILLA ATTACKED THE AUTOMOBILE DEALERSHIP BECAUSE HE WANTED TO ---

Now arrange the circled letters to form the surprise answer, as suggested by the above cartoon.

Print answer here

147

JUMBLE®

Unscramble these four Jumbles, one letter
to each square, to form four ordinary words.

ODWLU

NUBTL

PECIAE

ITOEMV

THE SQUIRREL WAS
STRESSED BECAUSE HE
SPENT SO MUCH TIME ---

Now arrange the circled letters
to form the surprise answer, as
suggested by the above cartoon.

Print answer here

JUMBLE®

Unscramble these four Jumbles, one letter to each square, to form four ordinary words.

ORHAD

RNOST

TINKET

QEULSE

AFTER REVOLVING DOORS WERE INVENTED, PEOPLE QUICKLY LEARNED ---

Now arrange the circled letters to form the surprise answer, as suggested by the above cartoon.

Print answer here

149

JUMBLE®

Unscramble these four Jumbles, one letter
to each square, to form four ordinary words.

ASCEE

TVEEN

EPPPRE

SLUEST

Don't even
think about it.

CLEAN UP
AFTER YOUR
DOG!

OWNERS NOT CLEANING
UP AFTER THEIR DOGS
WAS HER ---

Now arrange the circled letters
to form the surprise answer, as
suggested by the above cartoon.

Print answer here

JUMBLE®

Unscramble these four Jumbles, one letter
to each square, to form four ordinary words.

CETEJ

FAYTF

RABEBR

LUYRST

It has
everything
you could
dream of.

I can't
believe
this
place.

FOR
SALE

4
acres

It's
huge!

THE MANOR INCLUDED
GARDENS, A POND AND PLENTY
OF ACREAGE. IT WAS A ---

Now arrange the circled letters
to form the surprise answer, as
suggested by the above cartoon.

*Print
answer
here*

JUMBLE®

Unscramble these four Jumbles, one letter
to each square, to form four ordinary words.

PIYML

FRADT

ERBAWE

SANCIO

Our assembly
line has helped
keep costs down.

You're
brilliant,
Henry!

HENRY'S SKILL IN
REDUCING COSTS FOR
PRODUCTION OF THE
MODEL T RESULTED IN ---

Now arrange the circled letters
to form the surprise answer, as
suggested by the above cartoon.

**Print
answer
here**   " ◯ - ◯◯◯◯ - ◯◯◯◯◯◯◯◯ "

JUMBLE®

Unscramble these four Jumbles, one letter
to each square, to form four ordinary words.

USKOD

MRIPC

RSUYLE

GIRONI

Sonny looks great! He works out from sunup to sundown.

THE ROOSTER HAD BEEN
WORKING OUT AND THE
RESULT WAS ---

Now arrange the circled letters
to form the surprise answer, as
suggested by the above cartoon.

Print
answer
here

" "

JUMBLE®

Unscramble these four Jumbles, one letter
to each square, to form four ordinary words.

NCALK

OLAKA

RODFIB

DEXOUT

Let's head
back to the
cottage.

I'll
switch
sides.

THE CATAMARAN NEEDED
TO TURN AROUND, SO IT
DID AN ---

Now arrange the circled letters
to form the surprise answer, as
suggested by the above cartoon.

**Print
answer
here**

◯ - " ◯◯◯◯ " - ◯◯◯◯

JUMBLE®

Unscramble these four Jumbles, one letter to each square, to form four ordinary words.

UKKNS

BOTAU

GHALEG

EPSLIV

I feel like I lost around 5 or 6 pounds. Am I right?

Try the opposite.

HE PREDICTED HE'D LOST A FEW POUNDS, BUT WHEN HE WAS WEIGHED, HIS WIFE SAID ---

Now arrange the circled letters to form the surprise answer, as suggested by the above cartoon.

Print answer here

 "  "

JUMBLE®

Unscramble these four Jumbles, one letter to each square, to form four ordinary words.

VRIRE

SOYMS

DIDNHE

NLHECC

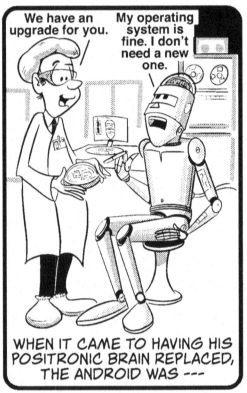

WHEN IT CAME TO HAVING HIS POSITRONIC BRAIN REPLACED, THE ANDROID WAS ---

Now arrange the circled letters to form the surprise answer, as suggested by the above cartoon.

Print answer here

◯◯◯◯◯ - ◯◯◯◯◯◯

JUMBLE®

Unscramble these four Jumbles, one letter
to each square, to form four ordinary words.

LYUFL

AEEST

GARULF

MNIOOD

Will you look at that!

Wow! It's so beautiful!

WHEN THEY SAW THE PARIS
TOWER LIT UP AT NIGHT,
THEY ---

Now arrange the circled letters
to form the surprise answer, as
suggested by the above cartoon.

Print answer here

 "  "

JUMBLE®

Unscramble these four Jumbles, one letter
to each square, to form four ordinary words.

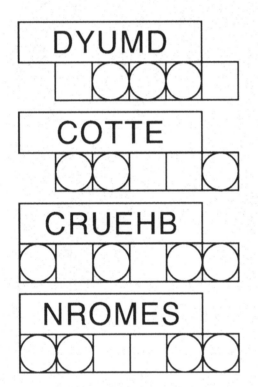

DYUMD

COTTE

CRUEHB

NROMES

CARPE LIBRE

We can't keep them in stock.

I can see why.

THEY STARTED PRODUCING
BOOKS WITH PAGES AND
WERE ---

Now arrange the circled letters
to form the surprise answer, as
suggested by the above cartoon.

**Print
answer
here**

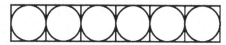

JUMBLE®

Unscramble these four Jumbles, one letter
to each square, to form four ordinary words.

NOCEL

WROFN

YEILSA

RREEGM

Take a
shower,
son.

Thanks.
I totally
understand.

I've got it
from here.

FOR THE STRUGGLING
STARTING PITCHER, BEING
REPLACED WAS A ---

Now arrange the circled letters
to form the surprise answer, as
suggested by the above cartoon.

**Print
answer
here**

159

JUMBLE®

Unscramble these four Jumbles, one letter
to each square, to form four ordinary words.

THAMC

PHEDT

CLIPDA

CETTED

HE REFURBISHED
BICYCLES IN HIS SPARE
TIME SO HE COULD ---

Now arrange the circled letters
to form the surprise answer, as
suggested by the above cartoon.

Print
answer
here

" ◯◯◯◯◯◯ " ◯◯◯◯

JUMBLE®

Unscramble these four Jumbles, one letter
to each square, to form four ordinary words.

CROGA

NTTUS

EYELKW

FCEDET

TALKING TO SOME PEOPLE
ABOUT CLEAN, RENEWABLE
POWER CAN BE A ---

Now arrange the circled letters
to form the surprise answer, as
suggested by the above cartoon.

Print
answer
here

JUMBLE®

Unscramble these four Jumbles, one letter
to each square, to form four ordinary words.

VIPTO

RNIDG

UFEEDS

LIDEUT

Is it
always
this cold
here?

Let me see!
It says, the
temperature
averages between
39 to 59 degrees
Farenheit this time
of year.

THEY WANTED TO LEARN
MORE ABOUT MOUNT
RAINIER, SO THEY ---

Now arrange the circled letters
to form the surprise answer, as
suggested by the above cartoon.

**Print
answer
here**

JUMBLE®

Unscramble these six Jumbles, one letter to each square, to form six ordinary words.

TFOINY

VTRIED

GEWLAG

RRHEAD

DONORI

MOLARN

I wish our budget was big enough to at least have trees.

At least we compromised with sod.

THERE WAS NOTHING SPECIAL ABOUT THE BOULEVARD'S NEW MEDIAN. IT WAS JUST ---

Now arrange the circled letters to form the surprise answer, as suggested by the above cartoon.

Print answer here

JUMBLE®

Unscramble these six Jumbles, one letter to each square, to form six ordinary words.

OSSANE

UNHAME

LYASAW

DILERV

FOTTIU

GEBINN

THE HOTEL AT THE BOTTOM OF THE GRAND CANYON WAS DONE, AND THE OWNERS WERE READY TO ---

Now arrange the circled letters to form the surprise answer, as suggested by the above cartoon.

Print answer here

JUMBLE®

Unscramble these six Jumbles, one letter to each square, to form six ordinary words.

GIDION

KULECB

GLERRA

DRIHAS

RULHOY

SALPHS

We're all going to clean the flower beds as a family today! Sound like fun?

Aww! We were going to hang out today.

I'm not thrilled either, boys.

THE TWO SIBLINGS EXPRESSED THEIR DISPLEASURE WITH THEIR FAMILY'S PLANS ---

Now arrange the circled letters to form the surprise answer, as suggested by the above cartoon.

Print answer here

"◯◯◯◯◯◯◯" - ◯◯ - "◯◯◯◯◯◯"

JUMBLE®

Unscramble these six Jumbles, one letter
to each square, to form six ordinary words.

WLONIF

SIYMDA

DOHWAS

CAVIET

MURSEM

SMECUL

IN THE LATE '70s, PAUL
DAVID HEWSON STARTED
GOING BY BONO AND ---

Now arrange the circled letters
to form the surprise answer, as
suggested by the above cartoon.

Print answer here

⬡⬡⬡⬡ ⬡ ⬡⬡⬡⬡ FOR ⬡⬡⬡⬡⬡⬡⬡

JUMBLE®

Unscramble these six Jumbles, one letter to each square, to form six ordinary words.

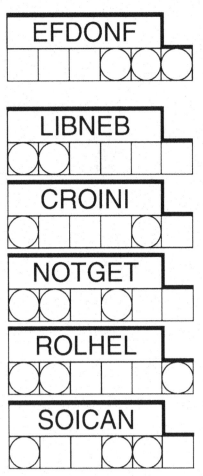

EFDONF

LIBNEB

CROINI

NOTGET

ROLHEL

SOICAN

JOHNSON FAMILY
HEATING & COOLING

All fixed, Dad!

What's with the new sign?

This will be my legacy.

WHEN THE HEATING/COOLING
SPECIALIST TAUGHT HIS
KIDS ABOUT THE FAMILY
BUSINESS, IT WAS ---

Now arrange the circled letters to form the surprise answer, as suggested by the above cartoon.

Print answer here

" ☐☐☐☐ " ☐☐☐☐☐☐☐☐☐☐☐☐☐☐☐

JUMBLE®

Unscramble these six Jumbles, one letter to each square, to form six ordinary words.

RAQSUE

HEYTIG

TRIPEM

PEBSUR

WDORAC

LEKENR

You'll need to get a job this summer to help pay for insurance.

Hopefully, you'll never need it. But we all have to have it.

I will.

HAVING CAR INSURANCE IS MANDATORY, WHICH MAKES IT A ---

Now arrange the circled letters to form the surprise answer, as suggested by the above cartoon.

Print answer here

" ◯◯◯ - ◯◯◯◯◯ - ◯◯◯◯◯◯ "

JUMBLE®

Unscramble these six Jumbles, one letter
to each square, to form six ordinary words.

CEKHTS

AAAPPY

GARFEO

AARTEK

REWLTO

TOSHOE

WITH *SO MANY RACE CAR
DRIVERS, 300,000
SPECTATORS, TV COVERAGE,
ETC., THE INDY 500 IS ---*

Now arrange the circled letters
to form the surprise answer, as
suggested by the above cartoon.

Print answer here

JUMBLE®

Unscramble these six Jumbles, one letter to each square, to form six ordinary words.

CCTHIE

IGNNNI

GMGSOY

SETNVI

SOUMTT

MLHEBU

Picture having two things and now, imagine you add two more things.

Aa Bb Cc Dd Ee Ff Gg

$2+2=4$

Can I imagine penguins?

TO TRULY COMPREHEND ADDITION, THE STUDENTS NEEDED TO ---

Now arrange the circled letters to form the surprise answer, as suggested by the above cartoon.

Print answer here

JUMBLE®

Unscramble these six Jumbles, one letter to each square, to form six ordinary words.

LNHETG

TAANSO

LYUPLE

AMLERV

TNIBET

GRIGEB

Grand Opening!

Let me get the games going with the first strike.

THE NEW BOWLING ALLEY WAS JUST COMPLETED, AND THE OWNER WAS ANXIOUS TO ---

Now arrange the circled letters to form the surprise answer, as suggested by the above cartoon.

Print answer here

JUMBLE®

Unscramble these six Jumbles, one letter to each square, to form six ordinary words.

UNCOPE

KEDRRA

MAAPLI

CROCHS

SITUHA

MICENO

You've always been my hero, Dad. Happy Father's Day!

You made a card for me. Just like when you were little.

HE WAS NOW TALLER THAN HIS FATHER, BUT HE STILL ---

Now arrange the circled letters to form the surprise answer, as suggested by the above cartoon.

Print answer here

JUMBLE®

Unscramble these six Jumbles, one letter
to each square, to form six ordinary words.

TNIKET

RALGVE

CDDOEE

TTHISC

NRIYEW

OMEBAN

Yeah, I'm going to need those reports now.

WORK ON RESUME

STEPLADDERS 2.00 SHIPPED
EXTENSION LADDER 2.00 SHIPPED

If you'd leave me alone for five minutes, I'd get them done.

THE GIRAFFE DIDN'T LIKE
WORKING FOR THE OTHER
GIRAFFE. HE FELT HIS BOSS
WAS ALWAYS ---

Now arrange the circled letters
to form the surprise answer, as
suggested by the above cartoon.

Print answer here

⬡⬡⬡⬡⬡⬡⬡⬡⬡ ⬡⬡⬡⬡ HIS ⬡⬡⬡⬡

JUMBLE®

Unscramble these six Jumbles, one letter
to each square, to form six ordinary words.

CAULTA

DMEIPE

SENTEL

CIHLGT

TRHEOB

PETTIO

I can see why everybody comes here.

Smile!

WHEN IT CAME TO DRAWING
TOURISTS, LONDON'S
FAMOUS CLOCK AND
GREAT BELL WERE A ---

Now arrange the circled letters
to form the surprise answer, as
suggested by the above cartoon.

Print answer here

JUMBLE®

Unscramble these six Jumbles, one letter to each square, to form six ordinary words.

NETOED

SLEUUF

CACURE

WREEPT

RFAMOL

CONOPU

I know we scheduled this performance last minute, but if we pull together, we can be ready.

TO GET THE SYMPHONY READY FOR ITS BIG PERFORMANCE, IT WOULD TAKE A ---

Now arrange the circled letters to form the surprise answer, as suggested by the above cartoon.

Print answer here

" ◯◯◯◯◯◯◯ - ◯◯ " ◯◯◯◯◯◯

JUMBLE®

Unscramble these six Jumbles, one letter to each square, to form six ordinary words.

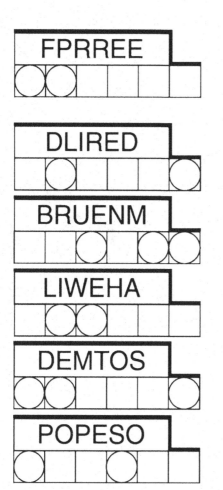

FPRREE

DLIRED

BRUENM

LIWEHA

DEMTOS

POPESO

It stores electricity to be used anywhere.

Brilliant!

He did it again!

What will he think of next?

WHEN EDISON INVENTED THE ALKALINE BATTERY IN 1901, PEOPLE SAID ---

Now arrange the circled letters to form the surprise answer, as suggested by the above cartoon.

Print answer here

JUMBLE®

Unscramble these six Jumbles, one letter to each square, to form six ordinary words.

FIDARA

MRIFON

MIKYPS

DARIEM

DYENOB

CENFIT

Cheers, to my lovely bride.

I'm so happy!

You two are so cute!

The food is so good.

I'm going to get some more wine.

THE WEDDING RECEPTION WAS AWESOME! THE NEWLYWEDS WERE HAPPY TO ---

Now arrange the circled letters to form the surprise answer, as suggested by the above cartoon.

Print answer here

◯◯◯ , ◯◯◯◯◯ , AND ◯◯ "◯◯◯◯◯◯◯"

JUMBLE®

Unscramble these six Jumbles, one letter to each square, to form six ordinary words.

DERITA

LRAFET

YSBLOM

CXDEEE

RHDYIB

CIPNLE

How do you get such great yields?

How often do you rotate crops?

Let me get you copies of my new book, "Let It Grow."

WHEN IT CAME TO GROWING THE BEST CROPS, THIS FARMER WAS AN ---

Now arrange the circled letters to form the surprise answer, as suggested by the above cartoon.

Print answer here

JUMBLE

Unscramble these six Jumbles, one letter to each square, to form six ordinary words.

HHLATE

YONMEK

TRUGET

EEEDCS

NOYERR

LUFOND

This tradition has been going on for hundreds of years.

Wow! That long?

THE CHANGING OF THE GUARD HAS BEEN A REGULAR OCCURRENCE SINCE BEFORE THE ---

Now arrange the circled letters to form the surprise answer, as suggested by the above cartoon.

Print answer here

◯◯◯◯ ◯◯ ◯◯◯ "◯◯◯◯◯◯◯"

JUMBLE®

Unscramble these six Jumbles, one letter to each square, to form six ordinary words.

GUTOHH

KIOBEO

TATHRW

NIFTIE

MUCSPA

TLANUF

THE SPEAR HAD JUST BEEN INVENTED, AND IT WOULD BE USED ---

Now arrange the circled letters to form the surprise answer, as suggested by the above cartoon.

Print answer here

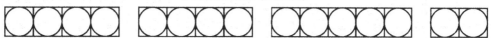

JUMBLE®

Unscramble these six Jumbles, one letter
to each square, to form six ordinary words.

GREATT

AAANBC

REEEFZ

JUTSUN

LITRLH

SASING

Here you see
cargo traveling
through the
Magellan
Channel.

That doesn't
sound right.

HE SAID THE BODY OF
WATER NAMED AFTER
MAGELLAN WAS A CHANNEL,
BUT HE NEEDED TO ---

Now arrange the circled letters
to form the surprise answer, as
suggested by the above cartoon.

Print answer here

JUMBLE®

Unscramble these six Jumbles, one letter to each square, to form six ordinary words.

TRIYGT

TOETAR

BEDSUU

PEUTEO

LOOLFW

BBHOON

We made it to the highest point!

We can't go any higher!

I wonder if they can hear you down at the base.

WHEN THEY REACHED THE MOUNTAIN PEAK, THEY REJOICED AT THE ---

Now arrange the circled letters to form the surprise answer, as suggested by the above cartoon.

Print answer here

183

Answers

1. **Jumbles:** SHYLY BEFOG LATEST PURPLE
   Answer: What jokes told by an abdominal surgeon are apt to be—BELLY LAUGHS

2. **Jumbles:** GIANT CLOTH ENCAMP SURTAX
   Answer: The artist went to the picture frame shop because he had so many of these—HANG-UPS

3. **Jumbles:** WEIGH EXUDE VERSUS FROZEN
   Answer: Why she liked the guy who always brought stale bread—HE NEVER GOT "FRESH"

4. **Jumbles:** DAISY AWARD DITHER FABLED
   Answer: Which side of the fire is the hottest?—THE "FIRE SIDE"

5. **Jumbles:** ARMOR BRASS NEGATE SUBURB
   Answer: What a backseat driver never does, unfortunately—RUNS OUT OF "GAS"

6. **Jumbles:** PANIC LOOSE CHALET UNHOOK
   Answer: What cap is never removed?—THE KNEECAP

7. **Jumbles:** ENTRY BRINY DRUDGE HANDLE
   Answer: What the formerly "heavy" client at the reducing salon said after she lost all that weight—"DE-LIGHT-ED"

8. **Jumbles:** OZONE CHEEK INDUCT MILDEW
   Answer: What the pillow tycoon got when business was bad—"DOWN" IN THE MOUTH

9. **Jumbles:** BANAL NOTCH SPORTY TRAGIC
   Answer: When prices on everything else went up at that store, envelopes remained this—"STATIONARY" (stationery)

10. **Jumbles:** CRAZY DANDY KOWTOW HALVED
    Answer: He spent his money like water but not this—ON WATER

11. **Jumbles:** TOOTH BLOAT LEGUME SCORCH
    Answer: Where grave robbers learn their profession—IN GHOUL SCHOOL

12. **Jumbles:** PAGAN YACHT COOPER NETHER
    Answer: What she wanted to hear when he asked her to share his lot in life—THE ACREAGE

13. **Jumbles:** JETTY BASIC EMPLOY AROUND
    Answer: When the diva got sick, her understudy grasped this—THE "OPERA-TUNITY"

14. **Jumbles:** CRACK SORRY FALTER PETITE
    Answer: Must have been a big wheel in the amusement business—FERRIS

15. **Jumbles:** SINGE FAUNA DISMAL BOYISH
    Answer: An angler either has fish lying about him or he's this—LYING ABOUT FISH

16. **Jumbles:** MOCHA NOISE REFUGE WHITEN
    Answer: An argumentative person is never so frustrated as when you do this—AGREE WITH HIM

17. **Jumbles:** POUCH FOCUS BETRAY DISARM
    Answer: If you have an itch to write, get yourself this—A SCRATCH PAD

18. **Jumbles:** OUNCE ARDOR MUSKET PONCHO
    Answer: That fanatic goes through life with a closed mind and this—AN OPEN MOUTH

19. **Jumbles:** RAINY PHOTO GRISLY INHALE
    Answer: What the recipe for this course requires a great deal of—"SHORTENING"

20. **Jumbles:** SANDY BASIN PLEDGE REBUKE
    Answer: In the spring the sky sometimes seems to do this—SPRING A LEAK

21. **Jumbles:** CANAL AIDED MISLAY TORRID
    Answer: What Dracula was looking for when he was driving on the small country road—THE MAIN ARTERY

22. **Jumbles:** NATAL BEIGE FRUGAL DEVOUR
    Answer: He was chosen to lead the crew to outer space, because he could be trusted to keep this—HIS FEET ON THE GROUND

23. **Jumbles:** WHEEL LOFTY BYWORD HOOKED
    Answer: How the bull showed deference to his mate—HE "KOW-TOWED"

24. **Jumbles:** GUISE LATCH IMBUED EXHORT
    Answer: What it was when he faked a sprained ankle—A LAME EXCUSE

25. **Jumbles:** PIOUS FEWER SHERRY CLUMSY
    Answer: What the politician was when the teleprompter failed to work—SPEECHLESS

26. **Jumbles:** DEMON VILLA FERRET BLITHE
    Answer: What she tried to do after she married that crude oil billionaire—REFINE HIM

27. **Jumbles:** DOUSE BLESS NOGGIN FEEBLE
    Answer: Before shoes can be bought they must be this—"SOLED"

28. **Jumbles:** WALTZ COLON MOROSE STUDIO
    Answer: Who saw the dinosaur entering the restaurant?—THE DINERS SAW

29. **Jumbles:** HABIT VISOR SCENIC PARODY
    Answer: There's a close relationship between a man's position and this—HIS DISPOSITION

30. **Jumbles:** OWING LOGIC POPLAR CLEAVE
    Answer: Meant the disappearance of the carriage—THE "CAR AGE"

31. **Jumbles:** CHAFF DICED GLOBAL JUNIOR
    Answer: A stick-in-the-mud found in a ship—THE ANCHOR

32. **Jumbles:** WEDGE BASIS PUMICE QUARTZ
    Answer: What tantrums are for some kids these days—QUITE THE RAGE

33. **Jumbles:** OCCUR STOOP PODIUM HYBRID
    Answer: When it comes to love, an engagement ring is this—A "BUY" PRODUCT

34. **Jumbles:** FRAME SOAPY QUEASY CHROME
    Answer: "Did you hear my last joke?"—"I SURE HOPE SO"

35. **Jumbles:** UNWED BOOTH EGOISM PEOPLE
    Answer: What a guy who acts like a heel should be—STEPPED ON

36. **Jumbles:** AMITY WRATH DENOTE SECOND
    Answer: What those young history teachers did at their annual get-together—MADE "DATES"

37. **Jumbles:** TYING CHAOS BEATEN WOBBLE
    Answer: How people saw things after the discovery of electricity—IN A NEW LIGHT

38. **Jumbles:** MESSY PURGE CRABBY HAPPEN
    Answer: What flatfeet can be—THE "ARCH ENEMY"

39. **Jumbles:** TRULY SWOON PUDDLE RACIAL
    Answer: What the Earth's two polar regions are—A WORLD APART

40. **Jumbles:** GNARL PRONE LIKELY TRUDGE
    Answer: A guy who has the right aim in life sometimes fails to do this, figuratively—"PULL THE TRIGGER"

41. **Jumbles:** STUNG CURRY FARINA JURIST
    Answer: What kind of an experience was it for the jinni to be in that bottle?—A JARRING ONE

42. **Jumbles:** BLANK MACAW CABANA WINTRY
    Answer: What the college halfback was in his studies—WAY BACK

43. **Jumbles:** DOWDY JOKER ASYLUM BEAUTY
    Answer: She had a steady job trying to keep him at this—A STEADY JOB

44. **Jumbles:** SUAVE ABIDE KITTEN HARBOR
    Answer: A golddigger is one who has what it takes to do this—TAKE WHAT ONE HAS

45. **Jumbles:** YODEL PORGY UNLIKE OBJECT
Answer: Could be a skeptic's outlook—A "DOUBT LOOK"

46. **Jumbles:** BALKY OXIDE FABRIC PLENTY
Answer: A businessman is judged by the company he keeps—PROFITABLE

47. **Jumbles:** LILAC POWER MAGNET BUNKER
Answer: That bore won't stop talking until you start this—WALKING

48. **Jumbles:** GOING ROBIN TYPHUS PYTHON
Answer: How he usually ended a sentence—WITH A "PROPOSITION"

49. **Jumbles:** FORUM LOUSY ADMIRE JACKET
Answer: What he got when he bought that "stylish" raincoat—"SOAKED"

50. **Jumbles:** ASSAY CUBIC SAILOR CRAFTY
Answer: What she thought that new freshman was—VERY "FIRST-CLASS"

51. **Jumbles:** SNOWY BEFOG SCHEME RELISH
Answer: What horsepower should be mixed with—HORSE SENSE

52. **Jumbles:** IMBUE FLORA WEASEL DOUBLY
Answer: What those newly hatched termites were—BABES IN THE WOOD

53. **Jumbles:** TOXIN KAPOK CAUGHT GRIMLY
Answer: Sometimes when the players do the running, the fans do this—THE KICKING

54. **Jumbles:** BASIS ENACT RABBIT AFLOAT
Answer: What some parents experience when they have teen-age kids—"EARITATION"

55. **Jumbles:** DALLY VERVE EIGHTY BEATEN
Answer: What many family problems are—ALL "RELATIVE"

56. **Jumbles:** HONEY LARVA WALNUT MORBID
Answer: If he starts right out complaining about her cooking, she'll learn better—OR HE WILL

57. **Jumbles:** PIETY RAPID UNPAID STYLUS
Answer: How many a "checkered" career ends up—IN A STRIPED SUIT

58. **Jumbles:** SURLY PHONY JUSTLY FALTER
Answer: Any man who survives by "doing nothing" is probably really doing this—OTHERS

59. **Jumbles:** ALTAR HOIST FLURRY PLAGUE
Answer: Why he was so popular in jail—HE WAS THE "LIFER" OF THE PARTY

60. **Jumbles:** EXUDE PARCH CORRAL FARINA
Answer: An outfit that makes one woman look slim often makes others look this—"ROUND"

61. **Jumbles:** TEASE CHALK EXCISE DREDGE
Answer: That so-called comedian had them "in the aisles"—HEADED FOR THE EXITS

62. **Jumbles:** SHYLY ELDER MUFFLE AUTHOR
Answer: They said she was beautiful but not quite this—"ALL THERE"

63. **Jumbles:** KINKY GLEAM VALISE AWHILE
Answer: One way to keep friends is not to do this—"GIVE THEM AWAY"

64. **Jumbles:** STAID POKER FENNEL TEAPOT
Answer: People who travel in order to become broadened sometimes return home this way—"FLATTENED"

65. **Jumbles:** PIOUS SNORT NOUGAT DEFINE
Answer: What could be more elegant than "eating out"?—"DINING OUT"

66. **Jumbles:** SUITE IRATE AFRAID MINGLE
Answer: It was supposed to be just a date until he started to do this—"INTIMI-DATE"

67. **Jumbles:** LOVER CASTE PONDER HYMNAL
Answer: To achieve a "triumph" in life, one must put these together in combination—A "TRY" & PLENTY OF "OOMPH"

68. **Jumbles:** FOYER PLUSH LAVISH BARREN
Answer: What he claimed he gave his wife—THE BEST "EARS" OF HIS LIFE

69. **Jumbles:** TONIC JOINT APIECE DISARM
Answer: Some people who think they're "operating" in the stock market are sometimes this—"OPERATED ON"

70. **Jumbles:** BYLAW ADAPT WEAKEN SUPERB
Answer: The pessimist had a happy look every time he had this to report—BAD NEWS

71. **Jumbles:** BATHE TYING DEBTOR ADMIRE
Answer: What she had when she met that eligible young bachelor—A "BRIDE" IDEA

72. **Jumbles:** FORTY USURP MUFFIN ENOUGH
Answer: Some people approach every subject with this—AN OPEN MOUTH

73. **Jumbles:** CRUSH BALMY INNATE MOHAIR
Answer: You're expected to make it in a hurry—HASTE

74. **Jumbles:** ACUTE WEARY JOYFUL KINDLY
Answer: All work and no play makes this—"JACK" THE DULL WAY

75. **Jumbles:** FELON BOWER WALRUS SMOKER
Answer: A wise man never does this—BLOWS HIS "KNOWS"

76. **Jumbles:** CHIDE LILAC DEPUTY QUIVER
Answer: Spend money like water and your debts will never be this—"LIQUIDATED"

77. **Jumbles:** BEGUN POACH CAJOLE SOIREE
Answer: What a fork in the road might have resulted in way back in those days—A "SPOON" IN THE CAR

78. **Jumbles:** WAGON IDIOM VALUED SEAMAN
Answer: Why some husbands think about running away to become outlaws—TO AVOID IN-LAWS

79. **Jumbles:** DOUGH GRIPE PUMICE WHALER
Answer: They used to call him the cream of fighters—until he got this—"WHIPPED"

80. **Jumbles:** WHEAT DAILY SUGARY FIRING
Answer: The horse you put your money on often does this—RUNS AWAY WITH IT

81. **Jumbles:** ABASH CHANT MISLAY UNFOLD
Answer: A stubborn man doesn't hold opinions—THEY HOLD HIM

82. **Jumbles:** MAIZE ALIVE QUAVER FIESTA
Answer: In addition to money, the rich never seem to lack this—RELATIVES

83. **Jumbles:** PEACE ROACH WINNOW MARLIN
Answer: They used to consider him a "rake," but now he's simply turned into this—A LAWN MOWER

84. **Jumbles:** YACHT MURKY UNLIKE FORGER
Answer: He build a good fire, and she said this—"GRATE-FUL!"

85. **Jumbles:** WOVEN SHAKY OCELOT HOOKUP
Answer: The boxing ring is no place for this—A SLOW "POKE"

86. **Jumbles:** DECAY QUEEN FLORID ELIXIR
Answer: What the stag did when the hunters arrived—RAN FOR "DEER" LIFE

87. **Jumbles:** ABOVE FLAME CALICO ENZYME
Answer: What the big dairy farmer had lots of—"MOO-LA"

88. **Jumbles:** DOWDY FAULT GLOBAL POISON
Answer: What she proceeded to do after her boyfriend canceled their date—BLOW HER TOP

89. **Jumbles:** CRIME FORCE PRIMED ENTAIL
Answer: He's supposed to be working at the dock for pay, but he prefers to do this—"FREE" LOAD

90. **Jumbles:** DIRTY QUEER VELLUM SEXTON
Answer: Why his conscience was clean—HE NEVER USED IT

91. **Jumbles:** FUZZY HUMAN AVOWAL DROPSY
Answer: What that buffet dinner was sort of—"LAP-HAZARD"

92. **Jumbles:** LIGHT AGLOW GIBBON INTONE
Answer: What some evening dresses are—
MORE GONE THAN GOWN

93. **Jumbles:** KNIFE INLET ABACUS GROTTO
Answer: Where the fanatic's train of thought always ran—
ON A SINGLE TRACK

94. **Jumbles:** CUBIC WINCE ENTITY AGENDA
Answer: Her promise to be on time carried a lot of this—"WAIT"

95. **Jumbles:** TULIP FAINT METRIC ALIGHT
Answer: Some people are tactful, while others do this—
TELL THE TRUTH

96. **Jumbles:** GLAND YOUNG EXTANT COERCE
Answer: What happened to those executives when there was a takeover at the food-processing company—THEY GOT "CANNED"

97. **Jumbles:** CROWN KNEEL LACING FIASCO
Answer: While on vacation some people work harder at loafing than they ordinarily do this—LOAF AT WORKING

98. **Jumbles:** SIXTY MINER PLOVER DULCET
Answer: A man usually can't think straight when he only has this—CURVES ON HIS MIND

99. **Jumbles:** FUSSY LAUGH BAUBLE GIMLET
Answer: He who indulges—BULGES

100. **Jumbles:** HONOR FLOOR DIMITY OUTBID
Answer: This might be more appreciated if we were given it later in life—YOUTH

101. **Jumbles:** DRILL ABOVE REMEDY DRAGON
Answer: Prices at the auction were going up and up. This would go on until the—"BIDDER" END

102. **Jumbles:** DRANK IMPEL MUTINY GALLEY
Answer: The largest New England state has 3,478 miles of coastline bordering the—"MAINE-LAND"

103. **Jumbles:** ELUDE SHEEN REMOVE PROFIT
Answer: The 2 was much more easygoing than the 3 because the 2 was—EVEN-TEMPERED

104. **Jumbles:** KITTY PIANO FUNNEL DENTAL
Answer: Olivia de Havilland would play Maid Marian to Errol's Robin Hood. She was—IN LIKE FLYNN

105. **Jumbles:** CHESS POKER HUGELY INSIST
Answer: The wealthy couple always flew first class and could well afford—SKY-HIGH PRICES

106. **Jumbles:** STAFF INKED RESUME RELENT
Answer: After upgrading to lodging with two bedrooms, they would have—"SUITE" DREAMS

107. **Jumbles:** THEME SLYLY PULPIT INJURE
Answer: She needed a blood transfusion. Luckily, the patient's boyfriend was—JUST HER TYPE

108. **Jumbles:** GOUGE GUPPY NOODLE SQUASH
Answer: When it came to tilling the soil by hand, he was—GUNG "HOE"

109. **Jumbles:** QUAKE NIPPY LAZILY DOUBLE
Answer: The blind taste test between the cola brands was a—POP QUIZ

110. **Jumbles:** BURST FRAME FALLEN GLOOMY
Answer: The "holes" on the Frisbee golf course were—FAR-FLUNG

111. **Jumbles:** LAUGH NUTTY COLONY FRENZY
Answer: The king hated his chair and wanted it to be—"THRONE" OUT

112. **Jumbles:** THUMB GAUZE ACCENT MYSELF
Answer: When the identical twins won the doubles tournament, it was—GAME, SET AND MATCH

113. **Jumbles:** FORUM DRAWL CANCEL SAVORY
Answer: It sounded like the crows sensed trouble based on the—"CAWS" FOR ALARM

114. **Jumbles:** NOTCH COMMA LAWYER CANDID
Answer: When the chef ran out of seafood for her famous chowder, it was a—"CLAM-ITY"

115. **Jumbles:** ROBOT VITAL SALARY FENNEL
Answer: How do you say action words such as give, accept, obey and untie—VERBALLY

116. **Jumbles:** CLEFT SPURN CLERGY WIRING
Answer: The small meeting of the shapes was called by the—INNER CIRCLE

117. **Jumbles:** DROOP EXILE STICKY BLANCH
Answer: The pennies were just minted and had a unique smell. This made them—"CENTED"

118. **Jumbles:** TIGHT THINK OUTFOX KENNEL
Answer: The number 1 is so low that its value is—NEXT TO NOTHING

119. **Jumbles:** COMFY MEALY INHALE ORIOLE
Answer: When making a new home, prairie dogs burrow with help from the—"HOLE" FAMILY

120. **Jumbles:** GLITZ GRILL TRENCH TATTLE
Answer: They wanted to install a new traffic signal and just needed the city to—GREEN LIGHT IT

121. **Jumbles:** STOMP VITAL MEADOW HOBBLE
Answer: The larger member of the deer family hung out with his cousins until he—HAD TO "VA-MOOSE"

122. **Jumbles:** HAVEN FATTY WILDLY SINFUL
Answer: Some people don't believe the Earth is spherical and—FLATLY DENY IT

123. **Jumbles:** MINCE SCOUT WEAPON HUMANE
Answer: The new clock they ordered would be delivered and installed—WHEN THE TIME COMES

124. **Jumbles:** QUOTA CARRY TEDIUM POLLEN
Answer: They arrived at the golf course early to use the practice green and—PUTTER AROUND

125. **Jumbles:** FLUTE SHRUG TENANT LOUNGE
Answer: They enjoyed the cruise's all-you-can-eat buffets—TO THE FULLEST

126. **Jumbles:** FRILL FINCH VOYAGE RUNOFF
Answer: When the winner of the marathon got into politics, he—RAN FOR OFFICE

127. **Jumbles:** NIPPY TOKEN GLASSY PALACE
Answer: When the restaurant charged 1 cent for its noodle dish, customers enjoyed the—"PENNY" PASTA

128. **Jumbles:** INPUT SENSE POMPOM TEACUP
Answer: After touching down on the moon, Buzz Aldrin told Neil Armstrong to—STEP ON IT

129. **Jumbles:** FLEET SWOON STRAND PELVIC
Answer: To rob from the rich and give to the poor, Robin Hood needed—NERVES OF "STEAL"

130. **Jumbles:** WINDY VIRUS BETTER WICKED
Answer: They decided to build their nest near the summit because they liked the—BIRD'S-EYE VIEW

131. **Jumbles:** SIXTY FORCE MINNOW TOWARD
Answer: He tried on the pants he wore on his wedding day, but it was a—"WAIST" OF TIME

132. **Jumbles:** KHAKI DRESS NOTION COSMOS
Answer: The collector who wouldn't stop talking about his model train had a—ONE-TRACK MIND

133. **Jumbles:** POOCH FROND TICKET WEAKEN
Answer: Failing his history test was a—NO-"KNOW"

134. **Jumbles:** NINTH PIXEL COARSE POROUS
Answer: As kids of cautious parents, they could only watch TV if they went through the—PROPER CHANNELS

135. **Jumbles:** BLOCK FAULT HOTTER METRIC
Answer: The podiatrist had a fancy new office and had enough patients to—FOOT THE BILL

136. **Jumbles:** LOWLY FRAUD COPPER SPOOKY
Answer: They wanted to make sure the locksmith's new website had enough—KEYWORDS

137. **Jumbles:** GRAVY NAVAL DISOWN MUSCLE
Answer: Construction of the subway tunnel was—UNDER WAY

138. **Jumbles:** ALLEY TEETH GENTLY FORGET
Answer: The hat made of matted wool fit perfectly and—FELT GREAT

139. **Jumbles:** MOGUL FRESH INVENT MELODY
Answer: Tightrope walkers ran in his family. He came from a—LONG LINE OF THEM

140. **Jumbles:** ENVOY DODGE SPOTTY TATTLE
Answer: The tennis player's favorite bagel was—TOP-SEEDED

141. **Jumbles:** GIZMO SOAPY MOSTLY INFLUX
Answer: For some wooly mammoths, the tar at La Brea in Los Angeles was a—PITFALL

142. **Jumbles:** LOFTY BURRO DEBTOR AMOEBA
Answer: The tourists enjoyed the view of the castle from the—"MOATER" BOAT

143. **Jumbles:** SWEET BISON STREWN PANTRY
Answer: The lawyer called the grizzly to the stand, so he could—BEAR WITNESS

144. **Jumbles:** SHAME PETTY HONCHO CLAMOR
Answer: The fashion boutique below her apartment was—"CLOTHES" TO HOME

145. **Jumbles:** PUTTY KNOCK PIRACY UNSAID
Answer: Godzilla attacked the automobile dealership because he wanted to—PICK UP TRUCKS

146. **Jumbles:** WOULD BLUNT APIECE MOTIVE
Answer: The squirrel was stressed because he spent so much time—OUT ON A LIMB

147. **Jumbles:** HOARD SNORT KITTEN SEQUEL
Answer: After revolving doors were invented, people quickly learned—THE INS AND OUTS

148. **Jumbles:** CEASE EVENT PEPPER TUSSLE
Answer: Owners not cleaning up after their dogs was her—PET PEEVE

149. **Jumbles:** EJECT TAFFY BARBER SULTRY
Answer: The manor included gardens, a pond and plenty of acreage. It was a—REAL ESTATE

150. **Jumbles:** IMPLY DRAFT BEWARE CASINO
Answer: Henry's skill in reducing costs for production of the Model T resulted in—"A-FORD-ABILITY"

151. **Jumbles:** KUDOS CRIMP SURELY ORIGIN
Answer: The rooster had been working out and the result was—GOOD "PECKS"

152. **Jumbles:** CLANK KOALA FORBID TUXEDO
Answer: The catamaran needed to turn around, so it did an—A-"BOAT"-FACE

153. **Jumbles:** SKUNK ABOUT HAGGLE PELVIS
Answer: He predicted he'd lost a few pounds, but when he was weighed, his wife said—GUESS "A GAIN"

154. **Jumbles:** RIVER MOSSY HIDDEN CLENCH
Answer: When it came to having his positronic brain replaced, the android was—CLOSE-MINDED

155. **Jumbles:** FULLY TEASE FRUGAL DOMINO
Answer: When they saw the Paris tower lit up at night, they—GOT AN "EIFFEL"

156. **Jumbles:** MUDDY OCTET CHERUB SERMON
Answer: They started producing books with pages and were—BOUND TO SUCCEED

157. **Jumbles:** CLONE FROWN EASILY MERGER
Answer: For the struggling starting pitcher, being replaced was a—WELCOME RELIEF

158. **Jumbles:** MATCH DEPTH PLACID DETECT
Answer: He refurbished bicycles in his spare time so he could—"PEDDLE" THEM

159. **Jumbles:** CARGO STUNT WEEKLY DEFECT
Answer: Talking to some people about clean, renewable power can be a—WASTE OF ENERGY

160. **Jumbles:** PIVOT GRIND DEFUSE DILUTE
Answer: They wanted to learn more about Mount Rainier, so they—STUDIED UP ON IT

161. **Jumbles:** NOTIFY WAGGLE INDOOR DIVERT HARDER NORMAL
Answer: There was nothing special about the boulevard's new median. It was just—MIDDLE-OF-THE-ROAD

162. **Jumbles:** SEASON ALWAYS OUTFIT HUMANE DRIVEL BENIGN
Answer: The hotel at the bottom of the Grand Canyon was done, and the owners were ready to—GET DOWN TO BUSINESS

163. **Jumbles:** INDIGO LARGER HOURLY BUCKLE RADISH SPLASH
Answer: The two siblings expressed their displeasure with their family's plans— "SIGHED"-BY-"SIGHED"

164. **Jumbles:** INFLOW SHADOW SUMMER DISMAY ACTIVE MUSCLE
Answer: In the late '70s, Paul David Hewson started going by Bono and—MADE A NAME FOR HIMSELF

165. **Jumbles:** OFFEND IRONIC HOLLER NIBBLE GOTTEN CASINO
Answer: When the heating/cooling specialist taught his kids about the family business, it was—"HEIR" CONDITIONING

166. **Jumbles:** SQUARE PERMIT COWARD EIGHTY SUPERB KERNEL
Answer: Having car insurance is mandatory, which makes it a—"PRE-WRECK-QUISITE"

167. **Jumbles:** SKETCH FORAGE TROWEL PAPAYA KARATE SOOTHE
Answer: With so many race car drivers, 300,000 spectators, TV coverage, etc., the Indy 500 is—A LOT TO KEEP TRACK OF

168. **Jumbles:** HECTIC SMOGGY UTMOST INNING INVEST HUMBLE
Answer: To truly comprehend addition, the students needed to—GIVE IT "SUM" THOUGHT

169. **Jumbles:** LENGTH PULLEY BITTEN SONATA MARVEL BIGGER
Answer: The new bowling alley was just completed, and the owner was anxious to—GET THE BALL ROLLING

170. **Jumbles:** POUNCE IMPALA HIATUS DARKER SCORCH INCOME
Answer: He was now taller than his father, but he still—LOOKED UP TO HIM

171. **Jumbles:** KITTEN DECODE WINERY GRAVEL STITCH BEMOAN
Answer: The giraffe didn't like working for the other giraffe. He felt his boss was always—BREATHING DOWN HIS NECK

172. **Jumbles:** ACTUAL NESTLE BOTHER IMPEDE GLITCH TIPTOE
Answer: When it came to drawing tourists, London's famous clock and great bell were a—BIG-TIME ATTRACTION

173. **Jumbles:** DENOTE ACCRUE FORMAL USEFUL PEWTER COUPON
Answer: To get the symphony ready for its big performance, it would take a—"CONCERT-ED" EFFORT

174. **Jumbles:** PREFER NUMBER MODEST RIDDLE AWHILE OPPOSE
Answer: When Edison invented the alkaline battery in 1901, people said—MORE POWER TO HIM

175. **Jumbles:** AFRAID SKIMPY BEYOND INFORM ADMIRE INFECT
Answer: The wedding reception was awesome! The newlyweds were happy to—EAT, DRINK, AND BE "MARRIED"

176. **Jumbles:** TIRADE SYMBOL HYBRID FALTER EXCEED PENCIL
Answer: When it came to growing the best crops, this farmer was an—EXPERT IN HIS FIELD

177. **Jumbles:** HEALTH GUTTER ORNERY MONKEY SECEDE UNFOLD
Answer: The changing of the guard has been a regular occurrence since before the—TURN OF THE "SENTRY"

178. **Jumbles:** THOUGH THWART CAMPUS BOOKIE FINITE FLAUNT
Answer: The spear had just been invented, and it would be used—FROM THAT POINT ON

179. **Jumbles:** TARGET FREEZE THRILL CABANA UNJUST ASSIGN
Answer: He said the body of water named after Magellan was a channel but he needed to—GET HIS FACTS "STRAIT"

180. **Jumbles:** GRITTY SUBDUE FOLLOW ROTATE TOUPEE HOBNOB
Answer: When they reached the mountain peak, they rejoiced at the—TOP OF THEIR LUNGS

Need More Jumbles®?

Order any of these books through your bookseller or call Triumph Books toll-free at 800-335-5323.

Jumble® Books

More than 175 puzzles each!

Cowboy Jumble®
ISBN: 978-1-62937-355-3

Jammin' Jumble®
ISBN: 1-57243-844-4

Java Jumble®
ISBN: 978-1-60078-415-6

Jazzy Jumble®
ISBN: 978-1-57243-962-7

Jet Set Jumble®
ISBN: 978-1-60078-353-1

Joyful Jumble®
ISBN: 978-1-60078-079-0

Juke Joint Jumble®
ISBN: 978-1-60078-295-4

Jumble® Anniversary
ISBN: 987-1-62937-734-6

Jumble® at Work
ISBN: 1-57243-147-4

Jumble® Ballet
ISBN: 978-1-62937-616-5

Jumble® Birthday
ISBN: 978-1-62937-652-3

Jumble® Celebration
ISBN: 978-1-60078-134-6

Jumble® Circus
ISBN: 978-1-60078-739-3

Jumble® Cuisine
ISBN: 978-1-62937-735-3

Jumble® Drag Race
ISBN: 978-1-62937-483-3

Jumble® Ever After
ISBN: 978-1-62937-785-8

Jumble® Explorer
ISBN: 978-1-60078-854-3

Jumble® Explosion
ISBN: 978-1-60078-078-3

Jumble® Fever
ISBN: 1-57243-593-3

Jumble® Fiesta
ISBN: 1-57243-626-3

Jumble® Fun
ISBN: 1-57243-379-5

Jumble® Galaxy
ISBN: 978-1-60078-583-2

Jumble® Garden
ISBN: 978-1-62937-653-0

Jumble® Genius
ISBN: 1-57243-896-7

Jumble® Geography
ISBN: 978-1-62937-615-8

Jumble® Getaway
ISBN: 978-1-60078-547-4

Jumble® Gold
ISBN: 978-1-62937-354-6

Jumble® Grab Bag
ISBN: 1-57243-273-X

Jumble® Gymnastics
ISBN: 978-1-62937-306-5

Jumble® Jackpot
ISBN: 1-57243-897-5

Jumble® Jailbreak
ISBN: 978-1-62937-002-6

Jumble® Jambalaya
ISBN: 978-1-60078-294-7

Jumble® Jamboree
ISBN: 1-57243-696-4

Jumble® Jitterbug
ISBN: 978-1-60078-584-9

Jumble® Journey
ISBN: 978-1-62937-549-6

Jumble® Jubilation
ISBN: 978-1-62937-784-1

Jumble® Jubilee
ISBN: 1-57243-231-4

Jumble® Juggernaut
ISBN: 978-1-60078-026-4

Jumble® Junction
ISBN: 1-57243-380-9

Jumble® Jungle
ISBN: 978-1-57243-961-0

Jumble® Kingdom
ISBN: 978-1-62937-079-8

Jumble® Knockout
ISBN: 978-1-62937-078-1

Jumble® Madness
ISBN: 1-892049-24-4

Jumble® Magic
ISBN: 978-1-60078-795-9

Jumble® Marathon
ISBN: 978-1-60078-944-1

Jumble® Neighbor
ISBN: 978-1-62937-845-9

Jumble® Parachute
ISBN: 978-1-62937-548-9

Jumble® Safari
ISBN: 978-1-60078-675-4

Jumble® See & Search
ISBN: 1-57243-549-6

Jumble® See & Search 2
ISBN: 1-57243-734-0

Jumble® Sensation
ISBN: 978-1-60078-548-1

Jumble® Surprise
ISBN: 1-57243-320-5

Jumble® Symphony
ISBN: 978-1-62937-131-3

Jumble® Theater
ISBN: 978-1-62937-484-03

Jumble® University
ISBN: 978-1-62937-001-9

Jumble® Unleashed
ISBN: 978-1-62937-844-2

Jumble® Vacation
ISBN: 978-1-60078-796-6

Jumble® Wedding
ISBN: 978-1-62937-307-2

Jumble® Workout
ISBN: 978-1-60078-943-4

Jumpin' Jumble®
ISBN: 978-1-60078-027-1

Lunar Jumble®
ISBN: 978-1-60078-853-6

Monster Jumble®
ISBN: 978-1-62937-213-6

Mystic Jumble®
ISBN: 978-1-62937-130-6

Outer Space Jumble®
ISBN: 978-1-60078-416-3

Rainy Day Jumble®
ISBN: 978-1-60078-352-4

Ready, Set, Jumble®
ISBN: 978-1-60078-133-0

Rock 'n' Roll Jumble®
ISBN: 978-1-60078-674-7

Royal Jumble®
ISBN: 978-1-60078-738-6

Sports Jumble®
ISBN: 1-57243-113-X

Summer Fun Jumble®
ISBN: 1-57243-114-8

Touchdown Jumble®
ISBN: 978-1-62937-212-9

Travel Jumble®
ISBN: 1-57243-198-9

TV Jumble®
ISBN: 1-57243-461-9

Oversize Jumble® Books

More than 500 puzzles each!

Generous Jumble®
ISBN: 1-57243-385-X

Giant Jumble®
ISBN: 1-57243-349-3

Gigantic Jumble®
ISBN: 1-57243-426-0

Jumbo Jumble®
ISBN: 1-57243-314-0

The Very Best of Jumble® BrainBusters
ISBN: 1-57243-845-2

Jumble® Crosswords™

More than 175 puzzles each!

More Jumble® Crosswords™
ISBN: 1-57243-386-8

Jumble® Crosswords™ Jackpot
ISBN: 1-57243-615-8

Jumble® Crosswords™ Jamboree
ISBN: 1-57243-787-1

Jumble® BrainBusters™

More than 175 puzzles each!

Jumble® BrainBusters™
ISBN: 1-892049-28-7

Jumble® BrainBusters™ II
ISBN: 1-57243-424-4

Jumble® BrainBusters™ III
ISBN: 1-57243-463-5

Jumble® BrainBusters™ IV
ISBN: 1-57243-489-9

Jumble® BrainBusters™ 5
ISBN: 1-57243-548-8

Jumble® BrainBusters™ Bonanza
ISBN: 1-57243-616-6

Boggle™ BrainBusters™
ISBN: 1-57243-592-5

Boggle™ BrainBusters™ 2
ISBN: 1-57243-788-X

Jumble® BrainBusters™ Junior
ISBN: 1-892049-29-5

Jumble® BrainBusters™ Junior II
ISBN: 1-57243-425-2

Fun in the Sun with Jumble® BrainBusters™
ISBN: 1-57243-733-2